Great Grilling

EASY & ELEGANT ENTERTAINING ALL YEAR ROUND

Hillary Davis

Principal Photographer MICHAEL GRAND

Grove Weidenfeld
New York

A FRIEDMAN GROUP BOOK

Published in the United States by
Grove Weidenfeld
A Division of Grove Press, Inc.
841 Broadway
New York, New York 10003-4793

Library of Congress Cataloging-in-Publication Data
Davis, Hillary.
    Great grilling: easy and elegant entertaining all year around/
by Hillary Davis.—1st ed.
    p.   cm.
    "A Friedman Group book"—T.p. verso.
    Bibliography: p.
    Includes index.
    ISBN 1-555-84264-X
    ISBN 0-8021-3270-7 (pbk.)
    1. Barbecue cookery.   1. Title.
TX840. B3D37 1989
641.7'6—dc 19

GREAT GRILLING
Easy and Elegant Entertaining All Year Round
was prepared and produced by
Michael Friedman Publishing Group
15 West 26th Street
New York, New York 10010

Art Director: Robert W. Kosturko
Designer: David Shultz
Photography Editor: Christopher Bain
Production Manager: Karen L. Greenberg

Typeset by mar + x myles Typographic Services
Color separations by South Sea International Press, Ltd.
Printed and bound in Hong Kong by Leefung-Asco Printers Ltd.

First Edition 1989

First Evergreen Edition 1991

10 9 8 7 6 5 4 3 2 1

I would like to dedicate this book, with sincere thanks, to Tim O'Brian, without whom I would never have been able to undertake such a project.

I'd like to extend thanks to my editor, Karla Olson, for her great expertise, her undying enthusiasm, and her faith in me; to Chris Bain for his eye for great photography; to Pauline Kelley at Zona for helping to gather all the props that set the style of the book; to Mr. and Mrs. Bernard Grand for the uninhibited use of their new kitchen; to Lisa Reade at The Barbecue Industry of America for her patience in dealing with my numerous phone calls and for supplying me with vital information; to may dear friends Katie and Andrew O'Connor for their tastebuds and invaluable feedback; to Michael Grand for his beautiful photographs, herb garden, and total involvement; to my aunts, Myrna Davis and Gloria Kamensky, for showing me Capri and sharing their interest in fine food and their good taste with me; to my parents, Laura and Hal Davis, for giving me the experiences that allowed me to undertake this project; to my childhood friend, Nancy Kalish, who opened the door and moved me forward into my career in food; and to Joan Seiden.

6

Introduction

8

GREAT GRILLING EQUIPMENT
Grills
Cooking Fuels
Essential Accessories
Suggested Additions

28

GREAT GRILLING BASICS
How to Lay a Charcoal Fire
How to Tell When the Fire Is Hot Enough
How to Tell When Your Meats Are Done
Tips for Grilling Meats, Fish, Poultry, and Vegetables

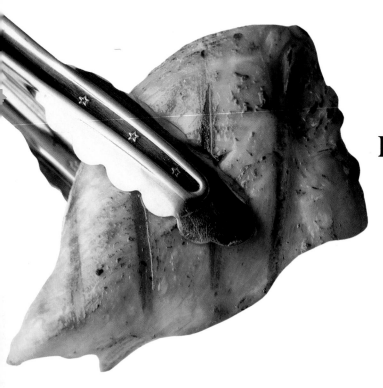

C O N T

40

GREAT GRILLING MENUS & RECIPES

115

Additional Great Grilling Recipes

121

Great Grilling Compound Butters

124

Conversion Charts

125

Sources

127

Index

E   N   T   S

*I*t would, at first, seem ironic that grilling foods over an open fire has recently become a novelty, for this was the very first cooking method. Cooking over charcoal, aromatic woods, and herbs has undergone a renaissance. Barbecuing no longer means only hamburgers, hot dogs, and ribs, although these remain the favorites of many people. Grilled food has become an integral part of *haute cuisine* and, more specifically, the new *spa cuisine*, and the most elegant and chic restaurants now feature grilled foods.

Thanks to the innovations of several chefs of the early 1980's, among them Alice Waters, Martha Stewart, and Wolfgang Puck, the word "grilling" has become synonymous with fresh ingredients prepared in the simplest but most flavorful way. The new health trends, which emphasize a diet containing less fat, have also encouraged grilling as an alternative to the classical cuisines that use fat ladened sauces, and even to the "lightened" style of *nouvelle cuisine.*

My own cooking philosophy has grown from a knowledge and understanding of all these styles, as well as from my own desire to live a healthful life without giving up the pleasures of good food. Use only the freshest ingredients when you are cooking, and keep it simple. This is the philosophy that I follow in this book. Recipes do not have to be complicated to be worthy of praise and appreciation.

My own enthusiasm for grilling generates from my love of food and eating. However, I am also concerned with staying fit and trim. The current trend toward healthy eating is here to stay. And grilling will no longer be relegated to the summer months, but will become more and more a part of everyday eating.

The use of fresh herbs in cooking has also encouraged my interest in grilling. More and more, grocery chains and farm stands are regularly carrying at least fresh parsley, cilantro, basil, dill, and mint. I also see that many more people—myself included—are cultivating their own herb gardens. Not only is it a delight to watch tiny seeds develop into mature plants, or to run your fingers through the leaves and smell the herbs, but also the freedom to experiment with fresh herbs brings depth to culinary experiences.

My passion for grilling began during my first trip to Italy. With my family everywhere we stopped to eat, a grill of some sort was being used to cook anything from wild mushrooms to whole roasts. Two meals stand out in particular. The first was in a hotel called La Badia. Close to Rome, the hotel was originally a

I N T R O D

thirteenth century monastery. It has been restored to a hotel but the original exterior of the monastery remains. It is set among hills studded with olive trees. The restaurant itself is dark, lighted only by a few candles and gas lamps. The main feature of the dining room is a deep, open stone hearth, wide enough and deep enough for someone to sit and tend the fire as well as baste the meats cooking over it, which are turned slowly by a weighted pulley. I watched the roasting of a suckling pig completely stuffed with fresh rosemary and encrusted with black peppercorns. The heat nursed this suckling slowly, and the result was one of the most delicious meals that I have ever had.

My second grilling experience took place on the isle of Capri at a restaurant described to me by my aunts as "the lemon grove" restaurant, but known in Italian as Da Paolino. We sat in the open under the stars and the gnarled lemon trees with their large ripe fruits, as big as grapefruits and as pungent as lemon cologne. Everything there was cooked on the grill, from small chickens to rabbits, and had been marinated in lemon juice and rich, deep green olive oil. The crusty, charred, and flavorful meats were so simple and unpretentious, and yet so delicious, that they made me want to duplicate this style for myself.

Of course, a dining experience is remembered not only because of the quality of the food, but also because of the atmosphere. When asked what I prefer, eating fine food or dining in a beautiful setting, I am extremely indecisive, for both carry equal importance. What I look for as a diner, a chef, and a host is balance between these two elements.

In *Great Grilling,* I hope to achieve a balance between great food and great style. Here, too, keeping it simple is the key. If the host is relaxed and can enjoy the party instead of spending all his or her time in the kitchen or over the grill, the guests will be more comfortable. The "Perfect Timing" section of each menu and the emphasis on advance preparation should allow any host to join the festivities.

In my mind, grilling is well on its way to becoming the alternative to a catered affair. Indeed, grilling, almost more than any other cooking technique, allows people to express themselves in their entertaining. I hope that this book will encourage you to experiment and to find your own style. I know you will have fun doing so.

U C T I O N

GREAT
GRILLING
EQUIPMENT

GRILLS

*F*or a beginner or a seasoned pro, choosing the perfect grill is a confusing experience. Because you've probably never had a sophisticated and versatile grill before, you will not be sure how much grilling you will be doing and what kinds of foods you will want to grill. Probably the only thing that you will be certain of is where your grill will be located, such as inside an apartment or outside in your backyard.

To begin, the best advice I can give is not to skimp on the type and durability of the grill you select. Do not choose a grill thinking that once you become more well acquainted with the grilling process you will invest in a deluxe model. If you do, chances are you will either throw this book and your grill away in the garbage, or you will go out and buy the more expensive model that you thought you would grow into. To avoid these two unsatisfactory alternatives, I begin my discussion of grilling equipment by describing the various types of grills.

Though they fluctuate in size, shape, and efficiency, grills, in general, are constructed in one way. They are all composed of a fuel bed with a cast iron, steel, or porcelain covered steel cooking rack above it. Variations include a range of shapes, attachments, levels of durability, and personal preference. Design and solid construction are of critical importance. Before buying a grill, check all moveable parts, such as vents, grilling racks, and hinges. With all grills, look for heat-resistant handles made of wood or durable plastic for easy maneuverability.

HIBACHIS

The most popular type of portable grill is the Hibachi. It is inexpensive and will easily accommodate a meal for one to four people. It is also terrific as an adjunct to the main grill for appetizers or side dishes. Being quite small it can be used on balconies or even within a fireplace. (Check with your fire department about safety precautions.) The Hibachi will grill to perfection with a minimum of effort and little

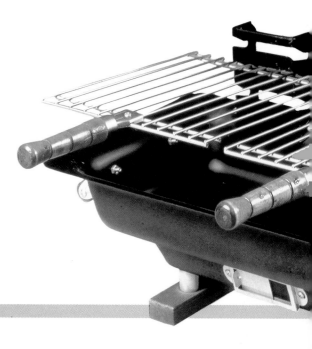

previous expertise. But its primary draw is that it is easily transportable to picnic areas, camp grounds, or football games.

Most Hibachis come with a ten-inch by fifteen-inch (25-centimeter by 37.5-centimeter) cooking surface, which explains the limited number of items it can handle. With the help of a conventional oven, however, you can effectively use a Hibachi to serve more than four persons. Simply grill the foods in batches, then keep the cooked food in the oven set on warm, or about 140 degrees F. (60 degrees C.), until all the food is ready to serve. At a picnic site or a campground, keep the cooked food warm in aluminum foil.

Many of the portable, tabletop Hibachis are miniature versions of the standard grill (some even look like covered cookers). They can be purchased in the charcoal models, as well as in the gas and electric models. One manufacturer offers a smokeless electric grill that can be used on the dining room table.

To use the Hibachi most effectively, place foods as close together as possible without overlapping, allowing very little space through which the heat can escape. Regardless of size, however, it does produce a high enough heat to sear meats, which helps to retain moisture and therefore tenderness. The Hibachi is a very manageable piece of equipment, and one can expect to cook on it with a minimum of fuss and bother.

DISPOSABLE GRILLS

A small note about the disposable grill is in order because they are so widely available in grocery and hardware stores during the summer months. Disposable grills have their obvious drawbacks and should never be used in place of more substantial equipment. However, if caught away from home and craving a grilled meal, I would not hesitate to use one of the these one-shot models. Some of the best dinners I have put on have been spur of the moment, informal meals. And so, when push comes to shove, I say proceed enthusiastically!

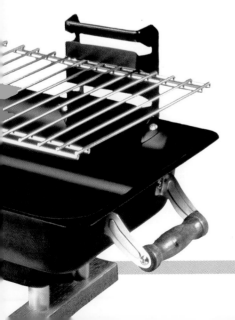

Just because you need to be careful when you are grilling, do not throw in the towel before you have started. There is no need for alarm. As with anything involving fires, it is important to take precautions and to be aware.

Find a barbecue spot out of the main traffic areas. The glow of the fire usually attracts people to the barbecue, but make people aware of where they should not be.

If you place your barbecue on a wooden surface or deck, place your grill on a heat-proof mat to protect the surface from burning.

Keep the grill away from a child's play area. Store lighter fluid and other grilling paraphernalia out of a child's reach.

CIRCULAR OR WHEELED GRILLS

These are usually round grills fitted with wheels for easy transport. They are often among the least expensive, but are also the least sturdy (except for the disposable grills). Since they are primarily open units, they are really only suitable for grilling quick-cooking foods, not more than an inch-and-a-half (four centimeters) thick. However, both these grills and Hibachis are equipped with a mechanism to raise and lower the grid, depending on how high or low a heat is needed to grill a particular food.

Some models are equipped with lids which make them suitable for smoking. Other models have electrically driven spit attachments, which come in handy if you will be cooking large cuts of meat. Some wheeled grills are designed for use inside; they are equipped with hoods and exhaust fans.

To increase a circular grill's cooking capacity, line the fuel bed with heavy aluminum foil, shiny side up. This will reflect heat off the bottom under the grid. If your grill did not come with a cover, simulate one by making a tent out of heavy duty aluminum foil. This will keep the heat in a contained area, resulting in a faster overall cooking time.

KETTLES

A kettle is one of the grills that I feel is most suitable for all-around cooking. Because of its shape, a kettle can be used as an oven, a grill, or a smoker. The rounded hood and bottom reflect heat off of all surfaces, which promotes faster cooking and a more intense, smoky flavor. The hood eliminates flare-ups because the hot coals are not exposed to as much oxygen when fat falls on them. The vents located in the lid and bottom further regulate temperature. When there is less oxygen let in there is less heat; more oxygen let in results in more heat. The heat is more even and controlled, allowing for a superior end result.

The disadvantages of kettles are that neither the cooking rack nor the fuel grate is movable, and the lid can get too hot to handle. Make certain that you always have a pair of heat proof mitts or pads on hand. Of course, these disadvantages should not be a deterrent to purchasing a kettle grill. Once you are familiar with its limitations, its advantages will increase in value.

HOODED GRILLS

These are usually square or rectangular grills with hinged hoods. The hood helps to trap heat for faster cooking and smoking. With the hood up, it acts as a regular open grill. Because there are pockets of air above and below the coals and grid, hot air circulates to the food. The advantage of this is that a more even heat is created, which means you will need to turn the food less often, and there will be a decrease in the consumption of charcoals.

Unlike the kettle-type grill, both the fuel grid and the rack in a hooded grill are usually adjustable. This will further allow you to refine your techniques and control your heat. Some hooded grills have fire doors through which you can add more charcoal as needed. Other models come with temperature gauges, which measure the surface temperature of the grid. There are a number of other attachments and the grills are available in many sizes and a wide range of prices. Because of their versatility, hooded grills are another good all-purpose unit.

In general, look around for dangerous fire hazards in your grilling area. Watch for dry grass, low-hanging branches, and wood-shingled roofs. Sparks may fly up into the air and land in unexpected places. Be careful, especially when using mesquite wood, which has a tendency to combust.

Place the grill about six to seven feet (two meters) away from flammable walls and at least twelve feet (three-and-a half meters) below ceilings or overhangings.

Courtesy Brookstone Co./Macomber, Inc.

KAMADOS

Kamados are oval, covered grills made of heavy clay that originated in Japan. Because they are porous and therefore hold heat, they are highly effective for slow barbecuing and smoking. However, they are quite cumbersome and difficult to clean. I do not encourage you to go out and purchase one unless you are mainly interested in smoking.

GAS AND ELECTRIC GRILLS

Although ardent grillers will turn up their noses at gas or electric grills, I feel that they are a more than adequate alternative to the charcoal-generated grill. Not only are they easy to get heated, but they are also a dream to clean and are extremely fuel efficient. All these things are making them increasingly popular today. Often in the kettle and hooded grill design, gas and electric grills contain permanent, briquette-shaped lava rocks that are heated by gas or electricity. They come in a variety of shapes and styles. I have worked in restaurants where we dealt with rather large versions of the gas generated grill. One of these, I recall, was positioned on an incline, which made it easier to turn hot food without scorching your lower arm. Few people will ever have the opportunity to use a restaurant-size or quality grill, but the home models are just as adequate for the kind of entertaining you will probably be doing.

The most obvious advantage to using a gas or electric grill is that you can maintain an even cooking temperature over a long period of time. This makes it easier to determine doneness of foods. Many still believe that there is no substitute for the flavors in foods grilled over charcoal or aromatic woods. However, in all honesty, I believe that it is possible to create similar flavors with marinades, or by adding water-soaked aromatic woods and woody herbs to the lava bed.

Gas and electric grills can be installed outside or inside. Many people I know swear by their Jen Air grills. These high quality indoor grills are usually sold as a separate unit that fits into the space of two burners on the stove. They are easy to use and easy to clean; all the pieces, except the electric rod, can be put in the dishwasher.

A couple of drawbacks to the Jen Air must be considered, however. First, the electric heating elements do not get as hot as you may want, especially for searing meats. In many cases, the cooking time must be extended, making it necessary to cook with a foil tent to conserve valuable heat. Second, like the Hibachi, the Jen Air does not have a large grilling surface, making it difficult to accommodate a meal for more than two people. If you have to cook on it for more than two, use the rotation system described earlier.

You will find that there is a significant difference in price between gas and electric grills. It is generally cheaper to buy an electric barbecue, such as the Jen Air, than to have a permanent gas grill with a tank installed. Gas tanks are unsightly as well.

However, it is possible to purchase an adequate and affordable portable gas model. In this case, the gas grill offers more efficient cooking than the electric for two reasons. First, gas—usually propane and sometimes butane—burns hotter than electricity. Second, gas grills feature movable lava rocks in the coal bed, where the electric model has only a coil. The lava rocks enable you to add aromatic herbs and woods to the fire, as you would with charcoal.

I once had a gas grill with a removable and refillable propane tank. I was skeptical when a friend insisted on using it during a blizzard. Astonishingly, she made quite a fabulous dinner despite the weather conditions.

For easy clean up of any gas or electric grill, line the bottom, underneath the briquettes, with aluminum foil. This will catch most of the juices and fats which fall to the bottom during grilling.

You will probably welcome people to help you in the preparation and cooking of food, but too many cooks can cause trouble. The solution might be to ask a friend in advance whether he or she would be willing to help, just to keep too many well-intentioned visitors from wreaking havoc.

Do not wear loose, gauzy clothing, especially in the sleeve area, for the material can easily catch fire. If you have long hair, it is a good idea to tie it back. If using propane or butane gas in canisters, be sure to store them in a cool place when not in use. When cooking, be careful not to place the grill near anything else hot, such as the oven. Propane is highly combustible and must be treated with caution.

SMOKERS

More and more home barbecuers are becoming interested in smoking foods. They are discovering it not as a substitute for barbecuing, but as an adjunct cooking technique. Many people refer to smoking as "true" barbecue. However, do not confuse these flavors with those of commercially processed smoked foods. These foods are "cold smoked," a method that cannot be achieved at home. Do not let this discourage you. Smoking foods is the gentlest way to treat them. It is a long, slow process by which heat and smoke both cook and flavor food. You will be fascinated by the tastes this method produces.

The *water pan smoker* contains a metal cylinder with either a pan of charcoal or an electric coil to provide heat. Halfway up the cylinder is another pan that holds water, vinegar, wine, fruit juices, or any other liquid you choose to flavor your food. Above this pan is a grid that holds the foods being smoked.

With a water pan smoke system, you can actually smoke, steam, or roast. The smoky fog generated by this smoker cooks meats while keeping them tender. This slow process requires no turning or basting. Large smokers come with several wire racks that make it possible to smoke foods in bulk. Some smokers have small side doors that allow one to replenish charcoal and liquids with minimal heat loss.

However, foods do not obtain the crusty exterior gotten from direct heat when they are smoked. This is one of the reasons that I do not recommend smoking as a regular grilling technique. A wonderful smoky flavor is easy enough to obtain by using a closed kettle grill and smoked wood chips, like mesquite or hickory.

If you want to try smoking foods, you can make your own temporary smoker. For one method, purchase three large, deep, disposable aluminum pans, fifteen inches by eleven inches by three inches (37.5 cm by 27.5 cm by 7.5 cm). Place one pan inside of the other,

© Michael Grand 1989

then fill the top pan with sawdust. Lightly oil an oven or cooling rack which fits inside these two pans, but which rests about two inches above the sawdust. Place the food to be smoked on the rack, then cover with the remaining disposable pan. Wrap a band of six-ply aluminum foil around the entire edge, where the pans meet, to seal in as much of the smoke as possible. Place the smoker over high heat, then when it starts to smoke, turn the heat down to medium. Leave on medium heat until food is smoke cooked. Some trial and error will have to be used to determine the smoking time of different foods. To give you a rough idea, it takes approximately twenty-five minutes to smoke a whole, average-sized Brook trout, and about five to seven minutes to smoke bay scallops. Be sure you do this procedure in a very well-ventilated area, or at least keep your doors and windows open.

Perhaps a better way to smoke foods at home is to construct a smoker that mimics the waterpan method. Usually these homemade units consist of a heating element at the bottom, such as a hot plate; a heavy metal or cast iron skillet holds the wood chips; a pan above this holds the liquid; and a wire rack above this holds the foods to be smoked.

I have heard of some people converting old refrigerators into these kinds of smokers.

RENTALS

If you should ever have to entertain large crowds, it is possible to rent grills large enough to hold as many as fifty large steaks. Look under "Barbecue Equipment" in the telephone book.

COOKING FUELS

CHARCOAL

Charcoal is the most widely used barbecue fuel, but it comes in several forms that vary in content, quality, and price.

Lump charcoal is produced by burning hard wood under special conditions that char it. As a result, it burns hotter, longer, and with less smoke than regular hard wood. Quite a few professional chefs who grill over coal prefer lump charcoal for this reason and because it does not contain any additives. Like mesquite, lump charcoal pops and sparks, so be careful when using it.

Most of the time, lump charcoal comes in a mixture of large and small chunks. By using it in this form you are liable to get a very uneven heat. To compensate, break the larger pieces into smaller ones, and try to use pieces that are uniform in size.

The more widely available *charcoal briquette* is lump charcoal stretched with fillers and binders. It is best to stay away from briquettes with a high filler content or chemical additives, since this seems to impart objectionable odors and flavors to foods.

HARDWOOD CHARCOAL

Hardwood charcoal is made from whole pieces of wood with no additives. The most common sources are mesquite, oak, maple, cherry, and hickory. Hardwood charcoal burns hotter and cleaner than briquettes and leaves no unpleasant taste or residue. Briquettes burn 200 to 300 degrees F. (100 to 150 degrees C.) lower than hardwood charcoal, thus requiring more briquettes over a shorter period of time. The hardwood charcoals also have the ability to be used two to three times more as well.

Mesquite has, within recent years, become perhaps the most popular hardwood for grilling. It is readily available and fairly inexpensive to use.

Mesquite wood grows mostly in the dry, hot climate of the Southwest and Mexico. Mesquite charcoal is derived by piling the wood into large mounds which are lit and allowed to smoulder for weeks under an airtight covering of clay and straw.

© Stan Sholik/FPG International

Mesquite burns very hot—at times too hot, which can char the food, causing it to lose its moistness and tenderness. Ideally, when grilling with mesquite, sear meats over high heat to seal in moisture, then remove them until the coals are at medium to medium-high heat to finish the cooking.

I find mesquite best in small doses. The flavor that it imparts is so strong that it can overpower even the most flavorful meats. It is a good idea to try a mixture of regular charcoal briquettes with mesquite briquettes. I have also gotten a good mesquite flavor with the addition of only mesquite flavored wood chips, which are added in small amounts to an already burning charcoal fire. However, mesquite wood produces more smoke than charcoal, which means a stronger flavor. Use it very sparingly until you determine how much of the flavor you like.

As I mentioned earlier, mesquite has a tendency to snap and pop. Make certain that the area around the grill is clear of dried grass, pine needles, and other flammable items. By using a combination of charcoal briquettes and mesquite wood, you will reduce the amount of sparking and improve the fire quality. Never use lighter fluid to light mesquite; the wood is so flammable you don't need it. Always keep a spray bottle, a bucket of water, or a garden hose nearby to combat flare ups.

Because mesquite imparts a very strong flavor, use it only with foods that can stand up to it. Some good matches with mesquite are steak, pork, lamb, venison, and oily fish such as bluefish.

Though currently most popular, mesquite is by no means the only flavored wood. *Hickory* has a smokier flavor than mesquite. Be careful that you use it with items that can hold up to its strong flavor, such as steaks, whole pork roasts, and fowl.

You can also use *alder, maple, oak, and cherry* to flavor foods. When using these hardwoods alone you should remember that they do not burn as hot or as long as charcoal. When you light them, allow them to burn until red hot and lightly covered with grey ash. At this point, start to cook, but since they burn more quickly than charcoal, gauge your time carefully. Use these woods with mild flavored meats such as chicken and veal.

Alder is a favorite in Northwest coast Indian barbecuing. It gives fish, especially salmon, a delicate wood smoke flavor and enhances the natural flavor of the fish, instead of overpowering it. It is also good for grilling pork and chicken. Alder comes in chips and chunks.

Fruit woods such as apple, cherry, and peach wood can all be used to impart a slightly sweet flavor to meats. To underscore the flavor of these woods, make a sauce using the fruit.

Grapevines give subtle bursts of heat and impart a sweet, wine-like flavor. They are becoming more popular, and more widely available. It is even possible to obtain grapevines from the vineyards of Bordeaux.

HERBS AND SPICES

For a special treat, experiment with herbs and spices. Try bay leaves or any of the woodier herbs such as thyme, rosemary, and sage. Try cinnamon sticks or whole nutmeg and cloves for an interesting flavor. Soak the herbs or spices in water for twenty minutes before you add them to the fire. Experiment with different herbs, using meats such as Cornish game hens, lampchops, swordfish, and chicken.

One last note: stay away from soft woods like pine, cedar, or fir, which impart a terrible flavor and coat your barbecue with resinous pitch that will be a real chore to clean.

ESSENTIAL ACCESSORIES

*H*ere is a list of all the culinary gadgets I feel make grilling that much easier. I have also made recommendations of what I feel is the most effective type of each accessory and, in some cases, when and how to use them. As soon as you start to grill with them, I am sure you will agree that these tools are essential.

THE FIRE STARTER CHIMNEY

This is another fairly reliable method used to start charcoal. The chimney is comprised of a metal cylinder with a handle and air holes on the sides. To use it, crumple one to two sheets of newspaper and place them in the bottom of the cylinder. Fill the

Courtesy Christen, Inc.

cylinder with charcoal briquette, light the paper, and within ten to fifteen minutes you can simply lift up the cylinder (use heat proof pads or mitts to do so) and pour the glowing charcoal into your barbecue.

The electric coil is my favorite technique for lighting charcoal, since there is little skill involved and, generally speaking, guaranteed success. The only inconvenience in using this method is the fact that you must place your barbecue near an electrical outlet or, at least, have an extension cord long enough to reach. If using an extension cord be careful to make sure your guests, especially if they include small children, are alerted to its whereabouts so they don't trip. Use the starter in an area where your guests—of all ages—will not venture. For further instructions and safety procedures, follow the manufacturer's manual.

CHARCOAL STARTERS

There are many kinds of charcoal starters, from lighter fluids to charcoal chimney starters. *Lighter fluid* is, perhaps by far, still the most widely used starter, though I do not recommend its use. Basically, you are pouring chemicals onto the charcoal. If you decide to use lighter fluids it is important to allow the coals to become eighty percent ash before cooking over them, or else the food may take on the flavor of the fluid.

If you use lighter fluid, keep the following things in mind. Use enough fluid to be certain that the fire will take hold; usually a half cup should do the trick. NEVER UNDER ANY CIRCUMSTANCES SPRAY FLUID ONTO THE COALS AFTER THE FIRE HAS STARTED. Accidents have happened where the lighter fluid has caught on fire in a stream from the coals back to the container, causing an explosion. Also, never substitute gasoline for lighter fluid; gas is highly combustible. Keep the lighter fluid in a cool place at all times and move it away from the barbecue while you are cooking.

Another way to start a fire is to place *newspaper* or *kindling* around the charcoal. When the paper or wood is lit, it will encourage the surrounding coals to catch. A great way to make newspaper kindling last a little longer in the fire is to roll one sheet of newspaper lengthwise, then tie it with a simple knot. Make a few of these and keep them on hand. Not only does this paper take slightly longer to burn, but it stays in one place without spreading over the coals and becoming a possible fire hazard itself.

Starting blocks are another alternative. They are small blocks made from compressed paper and wood with the addition of a flammable substance, usually containing paraffin.

SHARP KNIVES

The first thing one thinks of in respect to the tools of the cook's trade are knives—sharp knives without which the simplest slicing job turns into a nightmare. Much to the surprise of many people, it is the dull knife more than the sharp which is liable to cut you.

OFFSET SPATULA

A spatula is great for flipping fish fillets or whole fish. Make sure the one you choose is long enough and strong enough to hold the weight of a small to medium-sized whole fish. You should be able to flip it over or move it to another part of the grill without breaking the fish or leaving pieces of it all over the grill.

ALUMINUM FOIL

I am including aluminum foil on the list of must-haves because of its versatility. Although some barbecue snobs may turn up their noses at the idea of using mere foil, I still feel it is a useful tool for novice and accomplished grillers alike. It can be utilized to keep the grill clean, insulate, or as a cooking container. Heavy duty foil comes in a variety of lengths and widths. Keep at least a roll or two in different widths at your fingertips.

SPRAY BOTTLE

Whether a spritzer bottle, a mister, or a thoroughly rinsed old spray bottle, you should have a spray bottle on hand. You especially need one if you are using a Hiba-

© Peter Johansky/FPG International

chi or other type of grill without a lid, where periodic flare-ups are more likely. What happens when you have a series of flare-ups? The heat is inconsistent, which means meat is charred outside and raw inside.

SKEWERS

The person who invented skewers was a true genius, for I certainly can not imagine barbecuing without them. Not only are they good for holding small pieces of meat and vegetables, but they are also good for keeping food in place when it is turned or rotated.

It is a good idea to keep an assortment of skewers on hand of various lengths and materials. Choose metal ones that are square in shape, which helps keep food from moving around when turned. If you decide that you would like to use bamboo skewers, which are inexpensive and disposable, thus especially handy if entertaining a lot of people, soak them in warm water for at least half an hour before you use them to grill. This will prevent them from burning.

Toothpicks can be used to skewer small hors d'oeuvres. For instance, run toothpicks diametrically through sausage slices. You will have to use tongs to turn them. Serve them on a platter and have your guests pick them up by the toothpicks.

LONG-HANDLED BASTING BRUSH

This is a must, especially if you are brushing meats with a barbecue sauce or marinade. The long handle allows you to thoroughly brush the item being grilled without scorching your arm.

SERVICE SPOONS

Service spoons is simply a restaurant name for extra large aluminum spoons. If you want to purchase these, try a restaurant supply store or well equipped housewares store. Like the basting brush, service spoons aid in basting.

DRIP PAN

A drip pan is used to cook with indirect heat or to collect the juices from the grilled meat for an accompanying sauce. To set up your grill with a drip pan, mound the charcoals on either side of the drip pan, which should be positioned in the center of the grill bed. A nine inch by thirteen inch (twenty-two centimeters by thirty-two centimeters) pan should be sufficient. Replace the grill rack, then place the food to be cooked directly above the drip pan. Food is cooked by the indirect heat generated from the charcoals on either side of the drip pan. Grilling using this method will, in all probability, take longer, but the food will be moister and more tender. Juices released from the meat will be caught in the pan below and can be used in the preparation of a sauce, *au jus*, or gravy.

RAPID RESPONSE THERMOMETER

I recommend the rapid response thermometer made by Taylor. It comes in its own plastic case and can be attached to your apron or shirt pocket. It is the most accurate instant read thermometer that I have used since it has an adjustable bolt that can be moved to correctly calibrate it. You will find a rapid response thermometer most helpful when grilling roasts, whole chickens, chicken parts, and whole stuffed fish. To use one when cooking a roast, stick the prong into the thickest part, halfway between the bottom and the top of the roast. When cooking meat with bones, stick the thermometer close to the bone without touching it; this is usually the area that cooks the most slowly.

CARVING BOARD

I like to use a wooden cutting board with a trough around the perimeter. It is both beautiful and practical, for the trough will collect all the delicious juices. However, when using a wooden board, you must take some precautions, since it can be a per-

fect breeding ground for salmonella, a bacteria carried primarily in raw eggs and raw chicken meat that causes gastrointestinal inflammation and which can lead to death. Be careful not to place raw meat, especially chicken, on the board next to cooked items, and do not place cooked meats on a board which still holds residue from raw meat. Also, do not place any food on a board that has not been thoroughly washed. Lettuce and other vegetables eaten raw are particularly susceptible to picking up the bacteria from a dirty cutting board or knife. As a safety measure, always wash the board and knife with soap and water before placing a new item on the board or using the knife.

One option is to use a plastic board when working with raw foods, and save the beautiful wood board for carving and serving cooked items.

MITTS OR PADS

I personally prefer pads to mitts because they are easier to grab when you need to take something off the grill in a hurry. Whichever you choose, make certain you have at least two pairs or sets, and always have one with you when you are grilling.

SPRING-LOADED TONGS

Tongs are great for grabbing pieces of food, large or small, off the grill and for moving them to other areas on the grill. I find spring-loaded tongs much more manageable than the scissor type, which require some dexterity to operate, especially when in a rush.

STIFF METAL BRUSH

Before, during, and after grilling you will need a stiff wire brush. A grid covered with charred and greasy residue from previous grillings alters and very often inter-

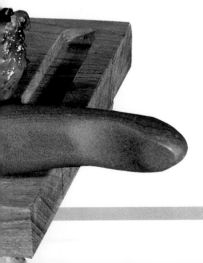

Bring one quart of water to a rolling boil. Hold the thermometer in the water without letting the tip touch the bottom of the pot. The thermometer should read 212 degrees F. (100 degrees C.). If it does not, the bolt behind the head of the thermometer can be adjusted with a small pair of pliers. Tighten or loosen it depending on whether your thermometer indicator is reading too high or low. When you adjust the thermometer in this way you can be sure you have an accurate reading. Measuring the temperature of the meats being grilled will make it easier to estimate your cooking time.

feres with the grilling process. Not only will it slow down the cooking, but the odors and flavors of what was grilled before will also cook onto the food you are grilling now.

The best time to clean your grill with a metal brush is while the grill is still warm. However, when grilling more than one food or grilling in batches, scrape down the grill in between removing the cooked food and replacing it with raw. Do not scrub too hard since you don't want to ruin the special coating of your grid.

SUGGESTED ADDITIONS

So far I have listed the equipment I feel you must have on hand for successful grilling. The list of secondary equipment, which follows, includes tools that will increase the efficiency of your grilling and broaden the kinds of cooking you can do.

GRILL SURFACE THERMOMETER

When you really want accuracy in your grilling, a grill surface thermometer will be a great help. It can be placed directly on the grilling rack above the coals to give an approximate temperature reading. Although you may feel more secure with the surface thermometer, I feel that the instant read thermometer is all you really need.

Some other additions to your tools might be: a ball baster, skillets, a cast iron pot for stews, electric fry pans, flash light, salt and pepper mills, paper towels, cloth towels.

SPIT ROASTING EQUIPMENT

Some grills offer optional electric attachments, and if you are interested in doing whole roasts, chickens, and turkeys, it might be a good idea to consider buying some of them. However, if you already have a grill, there are spits that you can purchase to accommodate this procedure.

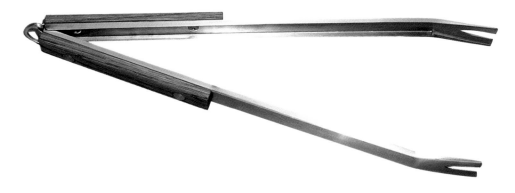

HINGED RECTANGULAR GRILLING BASKET

A grilling basket is convenient when grilling small pieces of meat and vegetables. It helps to keep them from falling through the grill bars or off of the grill completely. Anytime you use the basket, heat it over the grill first for five to ten minutes, then brush it generously with vegetable oil to prevent foods from sticking.

SMOKING OR FLAVOR CHIPS

I like using smoking or flavor chips because it is easier to control the flavoring of each dish. I liken it to seasoning your food with salt and pepper. When used in moderation, they give food a distinctive taste that is not overwhelming.

The most popular of these are hickory, mesquite, aspen, oak, maple, and apple. You can use them either wet or dry. You get more smoke from wet chips, which gives foods a much stronger flavor. Soak them in warm water for at least thirty minutes, then wait until the coals are covered with a light ash to add them to the fire. With a fireproof mitt or pad, lift the grid from the barbecue, and sprinkle a small handful of drained chips over the coals. Replace the grid and add foods, then cover the grill with the lid or make a foil tent for maximum smoking. You will notice that your cooking times will be longer since you are cooking over a low, direct heat with smoke. Be careful not to add too many wet chips at one time; this may create too much smoke, or may put out the fire.

FISH-SHAPED GRILLING BASKET

This is great for grilling a whole fish, especially one that has been stuffed. It works just like the hinged basket.

The most widely used forks for turning or moving meats on the barbecue are two-pronged. However, I find them to be quite ineffectual. In order to handle the meat one must stab it, which releases the juices and makes the meat tough and dry. If you can, use tongs instead.

GREAT
GRILLING
BASICS

Whether you are just beginning to grill or you are a seasoned pro, it never hurts to review the basics. In this chapter, I have included clear, concise instructions for how to lay a charcoal fire that is successful everytime. Then I have shared some tried-and-true chef's secrets for gauging the heat of your fire and the doneness of your meat. Finally, here are great flavoring and grilling ideas for all kinds of foods. With these suggestions, I encourage you to be innovative when you are barbecuing. You will discover that it is simple to come up with delicious new tastes. Experiment and enjoy!

© L & M Photo/FPG International

HOW TO LAY A CHARCOAL FIRE

*M*aking a proper fire is essential to great grilling. There are two basic methods which build a good grilling fire.

To prepare a brazier fire with charcoal, be sure to use enough coals to last through the cooking operation. According to the Kingsford company, it takes from twenty-five to thirty briquettes to cook a pound of meat. A twenty-six-inch (sixty-five centimeter) grill requires about fifty briquettes to reach a hot fire and maintain it for one half hour. A ten pound (4 and a half kilogram) bag of charcoal, which contains approximately seventy to eighty briquettes, will be sufficient for most grillers.

Line the inside of the fire bed with heavy duty aluminum foil to protect the grill and to make it easier to clean. Place the briquettes on the foil two deep or in a pyramid. For extended firing time, arrange an extra row of charcoals around the edge. These can be pushed towards the center as the coals in the middle start to fade.

To start the fire, use kindling, lighter fluid, or an electric wand, whichever method you prefer. Wait until about eighty percent of the coals are covered with ash by day or glowing embers by night to start grilling. These are the best fires because they provide constant heat.

The other way to build a fire is to pile the briquettes on the sides of the grill. With this method, you have cool space on the grid as well as hot spots, so you can move food around depending on how fast or slow it should cook.

A popular way to build this type of fire is to use a drip pan. First, preheat mounded charcoal briquettes. When they are eighty percent ash, spread the coals to either side of the grill. Place a nine-by-two-inch (twenty-two-by-thirteen-centimeter) metal cake pan in the middle of the fire box and spread the charcoal around it. You can leave the pan empty to catch any juices for a sauce, or you can fill the pan with liquid, such as wine or fruit juice, that will flavor the food being grilled.

Also, in this method, heat is coming from both sides, which helps tenderize tough cuts of meat by steaming as well as broiling. It also lowers the temperature of the grill to make a cool smoke possible.

HOW TO TELL WHEN THE FIRE IS HOT ENOUGH

*I*f you do not have a grill surface thermometer, here is a method that should give you a rough idea of when the grill is ready. Place your hand about an inch (two-and-a-half centimeters) or so above the grill. If you can not keep it over the grill at all, the fire is too hot. If you can count to three, the grill is very hot. If you can count to six, the fire is medium and up to eight, the fire is cool. The ideal fire for grilling is medium-high, about four or five seconds.

HOW TO TELL WHEN YOUR MEATS ARE DONE

*T*he chart on page 38 will give you an idea of what temperature the foods you cook should be when they are done. However, it is sometimes easier to test meats for doneness by touching the food. The best method I know is to use the firmness of your palm as a comparison; the flesh from the base of your hand up toward your thumb gets noticeably more tender. The base of the palm feels like meat that is well done. The area just below the thumb is like rare, and the area between the base of the palm and the base of the thumb is medium. While you are cooking, press your index finger into your palm, then into the meat. This should help you get an idea of what you are looking for. Nevertheless, even with this guide, this procedure takes practice.

This method is most likely to help only when you are cooking steaks, chops, and some fish. Stick to the instant read thermometer for roasts, chicken parts (especially legs and thighs), and whole fish.

© Ralph B. Pleasant/FPG International

TIPS FOR GRILLING MEATS, FISH, POULTRY, AND VEGETABLES

*O*ne of the most important things to keep in mind when purchasing ingredients for grilling is that you are more likely to succeed if you use the freshest and best quality products. Do not try to cut corners.

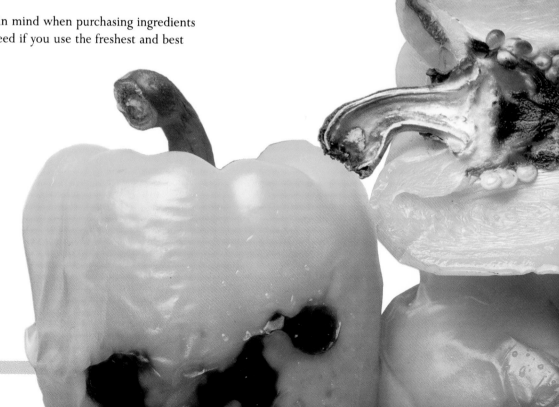

MEATS

The best steaks and chops for grilling are about one-and-a-half to three-inches (four to seven centimeters) thick.

The best beef to skewer is sirloin, but you may use less expensive cuts of meat if they are to be marinaded.

Trim meats of most of the fat. This will help decrease fat in your diet as well as help prevent flare-ups.

When coals have become good and white, lower the grid to preheat for about five to ten minutes. Sear steaks on both sides; roasts, on all sides. Searing—cooking the outside of the meat at a very high temperature for just a few minutes—will seal in all the juices. Then remove the meat until the fire is medium high; replace and continue cooking. Check for doneness with an instant read thermometer. When you remove meat from the grill, allow it to stand for about ten minutes before slicing or serving. As the chart indicates, on page 38, if you want a rare piece of meat, remove it from the grill when the instant read thermometer reads 130 to 135 degrees F. (55 to 57 degrees C.). Allowed to sit for ten minutes, the temperature of the the meat will increase approximately five degrees.

As the chart indicates, on page 38

PERFECT TIMING

You are having a party, but find that most of the time you are in the kitchen. You only pick up pieces of conversation as you pass from the oven to the table. I'm sure that any person who has ever had a party can relate to this scene.

With barbecuing, however, if you plan carefully, you can change your role from kitchen slave to partygoer. After all, parties should be enjoyed by all, not just the guests!

Try to do as much of the preparatory work as possible in advance, at least a day before. Make dressings, wash salad greens, cut vegetables, marinade, and skewer meats beforehand. Try to make grilling the only thing you have to deal with during the party. Chances are, when you get the fire going, your guests will congregate around the fire.

LAMB

A leg of lamb is great for a barbecue. Lamb is also good as shish kebabs and lamb steaks.

A loin of lamb or rack of lamb is also great on the grill. If the ribs of the rack are exposed, wrap them in aluminum foil to keep them from charring.

PORK

Barbecued spare ribs are, to many, the classic barbecue food. Before marinating and/or grilling, poach ribs in boiling water for about three to five minutes. This will help tenderize them and will eliminate a lot of the fat.

Try grilling whole pork tenderloins. They become as tender as filet mignon.

Marinade pork chops or grill them with fresh herbs in the fire. Pork chops are particularly good with rosemary and a piquant sauce, such as lemon, caper, or white wine, or a fruity sauce, such as apricot or chutney.

VEAL

James Beard thought it a sin to grill veal of any kind, but I disagree. If the right cut of meat is used and it is handled carefully, grilled veal is a wonderful treat. When grilling, stay away from delicate scallopini, but move right ahead with chops and roasts. Marinate veal chops in lemon juice and fresh rosemary. Stuff a veal roast with sage. Serve grilled veal with a sauce made from cold tuna, capers, and lemon juice. Grill veal over aromatic woods, but be careful when using strong ones such as mesquite and hickory. These tend to overpower the tender flavor.

POULTRY

Be sure to oil the grill with vegetable oil right before grilling any kind of poultry. Make sure the grill is hot. Both these tips will help to keep the chicken from sticking.

Have your butcher split whole chickens, as if for broiling, then remove the backbone and the end of the breast bone. This will allow them to lie flat on the grill.

When I am in a hurry, I precook poultry pieces with bones on high in the micro-wave for two to four minutes. This keeps the pieces from becoming charred on the outside, while remaining raw on the inside. It also reduces your grilling time by as much as twenty minutes, but does not violate the taste. If you do not have a micro-wave, precook the pieces in a conventional home oven, preheated to 450 degrees F. (230 degrees C.). Place the whole bird or the pieces on a baking sheet in the oven for twenty to twenty-five minutes.

Two hours before the party, start to assemble all your ingredients and your tools. Soak bamboo skewers in warm water for about half an hour before using; this will keep them from burning. Preheat your oven to warm

When buying fish to grill, especially fillets, ask for the skin to be left on. This will help to keep the fish in its natural shape and will make it easier to turn and move on the grill. The grilled skin is delicious, but it is easy to remove if you do not like it. Removing the skin will cut down on the fat content of the fish.

When stuffing fish, gently tie butcher's twine around the body of the fish to keep the filling from falling out, or pin the seam together with small skewers or tooth picks. Or use a grilling basket shaped like a fish.

Oil the grill before putting the fish on the grill. This applies to cooking whole fish as wells as fillets and steaks.

Small fish require a brisker heat than large fish because they are cooked for a shorter time.

If fish are very small, use a hinged grilling basket to grill them. Brush the basket generously with vegetable oil to prevent sticking, and preheat it over the grill before using.

so you can keep things hot as you go along. Most foods will keep warm in the oven for about thirty min-utes without altering the flavor or drying out.

Throwing fresh herbs on the grill when cooking fish is particularly good. Salmon, halibut, or swordfish are especially good cooked this way. Try them with marjoram, rosemary, or lemon thyme.

Fish steaks can be cooked in aluminum foil on the grid or right in the coals. Lay salmon steaks on foil, pour red wine over them, sprinkle with some vegetables and herbs, then wrap in the foil for a wonderful taste sensation.

Place clams, oysters, and mussels directly on the grid over moderate heat. Split lobsters, then par cook them in boiling salted water. Wrap them in aluminium foil and put them in the coals, or place them directly on the grid. Grill soft-shell crabs directly over moderate heat, and cook hard-shelled crabs like lobsters.

© Tom Tracy/FPG International

VEGETABLES

Almost any vegetable can be grilled, but those with a thick skin, such as eggplants, peppers, onions, and zucchini are especially good. Green beans, beets, and snow peas are a few exceptions, for their delicate flavor will be masked by the coals.

Root vegetables such as turnips and carrots should be parboiled, drained, then brushed with olive oil before grilling.

Corn can be shucked, wrapped in aluminum foil, and cooked on the grid or thrown directly in the coals with the husk still intact.

Grilled peppers are terrific. Oil the entire pepper, then place it on the grid and char it until it is black on all sides. Remove the pepper from the grill, and place it in a brown paper bag for five minutes, then peel. The steam released by the hot peppers in the bag will make peeling easy.

Ask a close friend or your partner to help you in the kitchen for a short while. Even if you do not need help, you will feel more relaxed knowing that willing hands are available.

Try to situate the barbecue close to an electric outlet, or at least close enough to reach with an extension cord. Do not be shy about using an electric fry pan to sauté vegetables or to make accompanying sauces while you are grilling.

GREAT
GRILLING

Allow plenty of time to preheat the grill. Charcoal, depending on the type of grill you have, will take anywhere from fifteen to thirty minutes to prepare. A gas generated grill will take about ten to fifteen minutes.

CLEANING YOUR GRILL THE EASY WAY

To me, the worst part of entertaining or just plain cooking is the cleaning up. With a few basic tips, however, grill cleanups are minimal. First of all, line the inside of the grill with heavy duty aluminum foil before putting in the charcoal or chosen type of fuel. This makes it easy to dispose of the soot and any remaining bits of charcoal or wood after grilling.

After grilling, but while the grill is still warm, use a metal brush to scrape off any residue or remaining bits of food.

It is even a good idea to scrape down the grill before you replace cooked meat with raw. Cleaning in between will increase the efficiency of the cooking process.

For hardened on or particularly messy grilling residue, spray the grid with oven cleaner. Make sure that you rinse thoroughly to remove all the cleaner. This is not a cleaning method to use every time you grill, but will help in very bad cases.

You will find methods for cleaning gas grids in the instruction manual, but most manufacturers agree that you should not scrub the surfaces with a wire brush, which might damage the special coating.

HOW TO SEASON YOUR GRILL

If the grid of your grill is made out of iron, it will eventually rust, espe-

cially if kept outside. You can minimize this, however, by keeping your barbecue out of the rain and covered, and by seasoning the grid.

Season the grill's grid as you would a cast iron skillet. Rub the surfaces of the grid with oil or shortening. Place the grid on a cookie sheet in an oven preheated to 250 degrees F. (120 degrees C.) and bake for thirty minutes. Turn the oven off. Keep the grid in the oven until it is cool, then wipe off residue shortening or oil.

HOW TO TELL WHEN A PIECE OF MEAT IS DONE

*T*here are two ways to tell when a piece of meat, fish or poultry is cooked as much as you would like—one is by internal temperature, the other is by time. The two charts below list the general cooking temperatures and times for different cuts of meat, fish, and poultry. Remember that these listings provide a range, generally on the rarer side of the spectrum. You can always cook food a little longer, but you cannot go back when something is overcooked. Therefore, start checking early, and you will be able to control just how well done your meat is.

When cooking roasts or whole meats, it is easiest to tell doneness with an instant read thermometer, which tells you the internal temperature of the meat.

For smaller and thinner (one to one-and-a-half inches thick, 2.5 to 3.75 centimeters) cuts of meat, poultry or fish, follow the minutes guide. After you've had some practice, however, you should be able to use the touch test described on page 32.

General Doneness Temperatures for Roasts and Whole Meats

Meat	Temperature		Notes
Beef	Rare:	130°F–135°F	Allow roasts to stand for ten minutes before serving.
Lamb Roasts	Medium:	150°F–155°F	
Veal	Well:	160°F–165°F	
Pork Roast		160°F–170°F	It has been determined that it is not necessary to cook pork until it is very well done to kill any bacteria in the meat. However, it is recommended to cook the meat past the medium stage.
Whole Chicken **Whole Turkey**		180°F	This time is approximate: cook until juices run clear when pierced with a fork.
Whole Fish		140°F	Cooking time could be anywhere from 15 to 60 minutes, depending on the thickness of the fish and whether or not it is stuffed.

General Cooking Times for Various Cuts of Meat, Poultry, and Fish

Meat	Time
Steaks (1 inch/2.5 cm.)	6 to 16 minutes each side
Burgers	8 to 15 minutes all together
Ribs	25 to 60 minutes all together
Flank Steak	5 to 15 minutes each side
Pork Chops (1 inch/2.5 cm.)	7 to 10 minutes each side
Lamb Chops (1 inch/2.5 cm.)	7 to 10 minutes each side
Veal Chops (1 inch/2.5 cm.)	7 to 10 minutes each side
Duck Breast	20 to 25 minutes all together
Chicken Breast	15 to 20 minutes all together
Fish Fillets (1 inch/2.5 cm.)	7 to 10 minutes all together
Fish Steaks (1 inch/2.5 cm.)	7 to 10 minutes all together

GREAT
GRILLING
MENUS
& RECIPES

© Michael Grand 1989

Crudités

Cajun Coleslaw

- ▪ *Baby Back Pork Ribs with Mocha Java Barbecue Sauce*

- ▪ *Grilled Corn on the Cob*

Peach Pie

Bock Beer

BABY BACK PORK RIBS WITH MOCHA JAVA BARBECUE SAUCE

For the Barbecue Sauce
2 tablespoons olive oil
1 medium onion, finely chopped
3 large cloves garlic, minced
1 6-ounce can imported tomato paste
3 tablespoons unsulphured molasses
¼ cup extra strong brewed Mocha Java coffee
¼ cup sherry
2 tablespoons Balsamic vinegar
1 2-inch piece fresh grated ginger
1 teaspoon Worchestershire sauce
1 teaspoon ground coriander
½ teaspoon cayenne pepper

*I*n an 8-inch (20-centimeter) skillet, over high heat, add 1 tablespoon of the oil. When hot, add the onion and cook, stirring constantly, until transparent, about 1 to 2 minutes. Add garlic and cook, stirring, until golden brown, about 2 minutes. Transfer to medium-sized bowl. Add the remaining ingredients to the bowl and stir until well-blended. Allow the sauce to stand at room temperature for at least 1 hour to develop flavors.

Makes about 2 cups

For the Baby Back Ribs

3¹/₂ to 4 pounds baby back pork spareribs

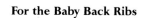
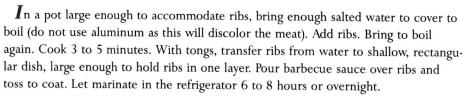

*I*n a pot large enough to accommodate ribs, bring enough salted water to cover to boil (do not use aluminum as this will discolor the meat). Add ribs. Bring to boil again. Cook 3 to 5 minutes. With tongs, transfer ribs from water to shallow, rectangular dish, large enough to hold ribs in one layer. Pour barbecue sauce over ribs and toss to coat. Let marinate in the refrigerator 6 to 8 hours or overnight.

Prepare grill. Grill ribs, slowly, over medium to medium-high heat. Cover with lid or aluminum foil tent for about 25 to 30 minutes, basting occasionally with sauce left over in marinating pan, until ribs are tender. Turn to second side and brush with more sauce. Cook 25 to 30 minutes, remove ribs to cutting board and allow them to rest 10 minutes. Cut into individual ribs and serve family style on platter.

Serves 4 to 6

GRILLED CORN

ON THE COB

PERFECT TIMING

The Day Before:
Make coleslaw and refrigerate. Precook ribs. Make barbecue sauce. Marinate ribs. Prepare crudités. Make peach pie.

The Day Of:
Prepare grill. Prepare corn. Make a large platter of crudité vegetables and serve with or without dip. Grill ribs. Remove from grill. While ribs sit, remove grill's grid and grill corn.

Urge your guests to eat corn without butter to get the full taste impact of the herbs.

6 ears corn on the cob
1 small bunch tarragon
1 small bunch thyme

Peel one side of corn husk away from cob without removing it completely, and loosen remaining husk. Do not remove silk. Stick branches of tarragon and thyme against the kernels and smooth back husk to original shape.

Prepare grill. Remove grid and place corn directly onto coals or lava rocks. Cover grill with lid or foil tent. Cook about 2 to 3 minutes. The outside husk will be charred but the inside will be steamy, hot, and tender.

Serves 6

Menu

Salmon Mousse with Lemon on Black Bread

■ *Barbecued Squab*

Wild Rice with Mushrooms and Onions

Steamed Baby Carrots

Poached Pears in Red wine

Wine: Moulin a Vent

---

1 cup very finely chopped scallions, including
   green tops
¼ cup honey
2 tablespoons Worchestershire sauce
3 large cloves garlic, minced
1 tablespoon dry mustard
2 teaspoons mild chili powder
1 cup Riesling wine
salt and freshly ground black pepper, to taste
4 6-ounce to 8-ounce squabs (have your butcher
   butterfly them)

*I*n a small saucepan, over high heat, combine all the above ingredients except squabs and bring to boil. Reduce heat to medium and simmer 10 minutes. Remove from heat and set aside.

Wash squabs and trim any fat from cavities. Place squabs in 9″ by 13″ (22.5 by 32.5 centimeters) glass or ceramic baking dish and pour barbecue sauce over all. Spoon sauce over so that all parts of the squabs are covered. Marinate at room temperature for 1 hour. Cover with plastic wrap and continue to marinate in refrigerator for an additional 2 to 3 hours.

Prepare grill. Place squabs on grill and cover with lid or aluminum foil tent. When heat is medium-high, grill 10 to 15 minutes per side or until juices run clear when flesh is pierced.

Serves 4

PERFECT TIMING

The appeal of this particular
menu is the fact that it is very
elegant, yet most of the items
can be prepared well in advance.

The Day Before:

Make marinade for the squabs.
Make the salmon mousse and
refrigerate. Cook the wild rice
and chop the onions to go with
it but keep them separate. Peel
the carrots and store in ice
water in refrigerator.
Poach the pears and chill.

The Day Of:

4 hours before you are ready to
grill, marinate squabs. Slice
black bread and keep in resealable plastic bag. Chop mushrooms for wild rice. Prepare
grill. Place squabs on grill and
put the bottom part of a
steamer with salted water on to
boil for the carrots. Cook the
carrots, and heat olive oil in a
sauté pan to cook onions, mushrooms, and wild rice. Sauté until
heated through. Keep squab,
rice, and carrots warm in oven
while eating mousse.

GREAT
GRILLING

*Baked Whole Garlic
with Crusty
French Bread*

■ *Grilled Venison
Steaks in
Red Wine Marinade*

*Baby Brussel
Sprouts*

■ *Grilled Polenta*

Apple Galette

*Wine:
St. Emilion*

GRILLED

VENISON STEAKS

IN RED WINE

MARINADE

© Michael Grand 1989

1 cup red wine, perferably Bordeaux
1 heaping tablespoon grain mustard
1 tablespoon chopped fresh thyme
2 bay leaves
12 black peppercorns, crushed
2 teaspoons salt
4 to 6 6-ounce venison steaks

Combine wine, mustard, thyme, bay leaves, peppercorns, and salt together in a large bowl. Mix well. Add venison steaks and toss to coat. Cover bowl with plastic wrap and marinate 8 hours or overnight. Remove venison from refrigerator 1 hour before you are ready to grill. Drain marinade just before grilling. Prepare grill. When heat is medium-high, place steaks on grill. Sear 2 to 3 minutes on each side to seal in juices. Remove from grill until heat is medium, then replace and continue cooking 3 to 5 minutes longer on each side or until desired doneness.

Makes 2 cups marinade
Serves 4 to 6

GRILLED POLENTA
WITH PINE NUTS
AND BASIL

7 cups water
$\frac{1}{2}$ teaspoon salt
1 $\frac{2}{3}$ cup cornmeal
$\frac{1}{2}$ cup chopped fresh basil
$\frac{1}{2}$ cup toasted and chopped pine nuts
$\frac{1}{2}$ cup freshly grated parmesan cheese
olive oil

*P*reheat oven to 350 degrees F. (175 degrees C.). In a 3-quart (3-liter) pot, add water and salt. Bring to boil over high heat. Slowly, in a thin stream, add cornmeal, stirring constantly. Reduce heat to medium-high and continue cooking for about 35 to 40 minutes or until mixture begins to leave the sides of the pan. Remove from heat. Stir in basil, pine nuts, and parmesan cheese. Mix thoroughly to evenly distribute.

Oil a shallow 11″ by 9″ (27.5 cm by 22.5 cm) baking pan. Spread polenta mixture on bottom of pan. Cover pan with aluminum foil and bake for about 15 minutes or until firmly set. Remove from oven and cool.

Cut into diamond shapes or use cookie cutters in desired shapes. Transfer shapes to oiled cookie sheet.

Prepare grill. When medium hot, brush each piece of polenta generously with olive oil and grill 2 to 3 minutes on each side until golden brown.

Makes about 25 triangles
Serves 6 to 8

PERFECT TIMING

The Day Before:

Make marinade and marinate venison. Clean and make cross mark in the bottom of each brussel sprout for more even cooking. Bake polenta and cut into diamonds or other shapes. Cover and refrigerate.

The Day Of:

In the morning, make the apple galette and keep it at room temperature. Prepare grill. 45 minutes before you are ready to grill the venison, bake the garlic and slice the french bread. Bring salted water to boil and cook brussel sprouts about 7 to 10 minutes or until fork tender. Drain and keep warm in oven if necessary. Grill steaks until desired doneness. Keep warm in oven with sprouts while grilling polenta. Grill polenta.

- *Grilled Eggplant with Sesame Sauce*

- *Grilled Spiced Cornish Game Hens*

Steamed Spinach

Wheat Pilaf

Hazelnut Torte

Wine: Sancerre

GRILLED EGGPLANT

WITH

SESAME SAUCE

© Robert Lima/Envision

2 large eggplants
¼ cup teriyaki sauce
2 tablespoons sesame oil
3 tablespoons Mirin wine
2 tablespoons light Oriental soy bean paste*
2 tablespoons black soy sauce*
2 tablespoons minced green part of scallion
1 tablespoon granulated sugar
4 medium cloves garlic, minced
2-inch piece fresh ginger, peeled and minced
2 teaspoons hot chili paste with garlic*
2 tablespoons sesame seeds, toasted

*T*rim ends off eggplant, but do not pare. Cut each eggplant in half lengthwise and cut each half into 1-inch (2½ centimeters) thick slices. Salt the eggplant slices, place them in a colander over the sink and drain for 30 minutes.

Meanwhile, in a large mixing bowl, combine teriyaki sauce, sesame oil, Mirin, soy bean paste, black soy, scallions, sugar, garlic, ginger, and chili paste. Blend well and reserve.

Rinse eggplant slices and add them to the marinade. Marinate for 3 to 4 hours, tossing occasionally.

Prepare grill. When heat is high, place eggplant slices on grid. Cook 3 to 5 minutes on each side or until eggplant is tender and golden. Transfer cooked eggplant to a warm serving platter, pour any remaining marinade over top and sprinkle with toasted sesame seeds.

Serves 4 to 6

*Note: These ingredients can be found in most oriental grocery stores.

GRILLED SPICED

CORNISH GAME

HENS

3 Cornish game hens, split, breast bone removed
   and halved
4 large cloves garlic, crushed
1 4-inch piece fresh ginger, peeled and finely
   minced
3 tablespoons anise seed, toasted
1 teaspoon finely chopped saffron threads
1 tablespoon paprika
1 teaspoon cayenne pepper
$1/2$ cup freshly squeezed lemon juice
1 large bunch coriander, chopped
2 scallions, chopped
$1/2$ cup extra virgin olive oil
$1/2$ cup vegetable oil

PERFECT TIMING

The Day Before:
Make hazelnut torte. Marinate
Cornish game hens. Clean and
wash spinach. Make marinade
for eggplant. Toast sesame seeds.

The Day Of:
Cut and salt eggplant. Rinse
after 30 minutes and place egg-
plant in marinade. Prepare grill.
Grill eggplant and sprinkle with
sesame seeds. Grill hens. 20
minutes before hens are cooked,
heat water or chicken broth for
wheat pilaf. Cook pilaf. 5 min-
utes before ready to serve hens,
steam spinach.

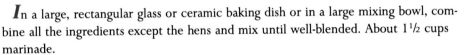

*I*n a large, rectangular glass or ceramic baking dish or in a large mixing bowl, combine all the ingredients except the hens and mix until well-blended. About $1 1/2$ cups
marinade.

   Add hens to marinade and toss to coat. Cover with plastic wrap and marinate overnight in refrigerator. Toss occasionally.

   Prepare grill. Sear hens over high heat for 3 to 5 minutes on each side. Remove and
allow grill to cool to medium-high. Place hens on grid and cook, covered, 25 to 30
minutes or until juices run clear when cut into.

Serves 6

© Michael Grand 1989

Purée of Carrot and Ginger Soup

■ Grilled Salmon Fillets with Salsa Cruda and Sautéed Arugula

Parsleyed New Potatoes

Raspberry Mousse

Wine:
Rose D'Anjou

GRILLED SALMON

WITH SALSA

CRUDA AND

SAUTÉED ARUGULA

For the Salsa
5 large ripe tomatoes, peeled, seeded, and
 chopped
2 large cloves garlic, minced
2 tablespoons chopped fresh cilantro
1 Jalapeño pepper, seeded and finely chopped
¼ cup freshly squeezed lime juice
3 tablespoons red wine vinegar
1 teaspoon fine sea salt
½ teaspoon freshly ground black pepper
¼ teaspoon hot red pepper sauce

*I*n a 3-quart (3-liter) sauce pan, bring 2 quarts salted water to boil over high heat. Core tomatoes and with the knife tip make a cross in the underside of the tomatoes' skin. When water is boiling add tomatoes for about 1 minute. Transfer them to a bowl filled with ice water. When all the tomatoes have been blanched, peel them, cut them in half from top to bottom, and gently squeeze out seeds. Chop roughly and place in medium-sized mixing bowl. Add rest of ingredients and mix thoroughly. Let sit at room temperature for at least 1 hour to blend flavors.

Makes about 2½ cups salsa

For the Salmon
4 to 6 ½-pound fillets of salmon with skin
vegetable oil
salt and pepper, to taste

*P*repare grill. When heat is medium-high, brush salmon generously with the vegetable oil and season with salt and pepper to taste, then place salmon on grill, skin side up. Cover with grill lid or aluminum foil tent and cook about 5 to 7 minutes. Remove lid, turn to second side, and cover again. Cook an additional 5 to 7 minutes or until desired doneness. When salmon is cooked, transfer it to oven-proof platter and keep warm in oven while sautéeing arugula.

For the Arugula
2 large bunches fresh arugula, trimmed and
    washed
3 tablespoons extra virgin olive oil
salt and black pepper, to taste

*I*n a 12-inch sauté pan, over low heat, add olive oil. When olive oil begins to get just slightly warm, about 1 to 2 minutes, remove pan from heat. Add arugula and toss until it is slightly wilted. Do not wilt arugula too much. You simply want to warm it. Season with salt and pepper to taste.

   To serve, place about 2 to 3 large tablespoons of salsa in the middle of each plate. Spread the sauce to the edges of the plate using the back of a spoon. Place salmon fillet in center and arrange wilted arugula around perimeter of plate. Serve immediately.

Serves 4 to 6

© Robert Lima/Envision

PERFECT TIMING

The Day Before:
Make carrot and ginger soup and keep refrigerated. Make salsa cruda and refrigerate. Make raspberry mousse and set to chill in dessert or champagne glasses. Wash arugula and dry with paper towel. Place in resealable plastic bag and refrigerate. Chop parsley.

The Day Of:
Prepare grill. 30 minutes before grilling fish, heat soup and bring new potatoes to boil in salted water. Cook potatoes until tender. Remove from heat, drain, and cover until ready to serve. Serve soup. Add salmon to grill. 2 minutes before salmon is ready, heat large skillet for arugula. Prepare plates with salsa and salmon. Add arugula to skillet as directed. Place arugula on plate as directed. Sprinkle potatoes with parsley and serve.

© Amy Reichman/Envision

Menu

Guacamole with Spicy Corn Chips

■ *Fajites*

Corn Bread

Margarita Pie

Mexican Coffee

Sangria or Dos Equis Beer

---

4 to 5 large cloves garlic, crushed
¹/₄ cup freshly squeezed lime juice
2 teaspoons salt
1 tablespoon chili powder
¹/₂ teaspoon hot red pepper flakes
¹/₂ cup Balsamic vinegar
2 tablespoons soy sauce
¹/₄ cup chopped fresh cilantro
2 pounds skirt or flank steak
6-8 tortillas
shredded lettuce
guacamole or avocado, peeled, pit removed, and diced
salsa
sour cream

Combine all of the above ingredients except steak in a shallow 9″ by 13″ (2.5 cm by 32.5 cm) glass or ceramic baking dish. Blend thoroughly with wire whisk. Add steak in one layer (you may have to cut it in half so that it fits).

Toss to coat so meat is completely covered by marinade. Cover with plastic wrap. Refrigerate for 6 hours or over night.

Prepare grill. Grill steak over high heat 3 to 5 minutes on each side or until desired doneness. Remove to cutting board and let sit 10 minutes. Slice thinly.

To assemble, layer the center of a warmed tortilla with shredded lettuce, top with sliced steak. Sprinkle steak with guacamole, salsa, and sour cream. Roll tortilla and eat with your hands.

About 1 cup marinade
Serves 6 to 8

PERFECT TIMING

The Day Before:
Make guacamole, salsa, and your own tortilla chips spiced with hot chile powder and/or cayenne pepper. Make marinade and marinate fajites. Make margarita pie.

The Day Of:
Make the cornbread about 1 hour before ready to grill so that it is still warm when ready to eat. Prepare grill. Grill steak.

© Michael Grand 1989

© Michael Grand 1989

GREAT
GRILLING

YAKETORI

- **Chicken Yaketori**

- **Sesame Swordfish Kebobs**

Sautéed Snow Peas with Ginger and Water Chestnuts

Short Grained Brown Rice

Seasonal Fruit Salad

Lapsang Souchong Tea

Wine: Soave

1 large clove garlic, minced
1 2-inch piece fresh ginger, peeled and minced
1/4 cup Mirin wine
1/2 cup white wine vinegar
1 tablespoon soy sauce
1 tablespoon sesame oil
1/2 cup vegetable oil
2 tablespoons dry sherry
4 chicken breasts, boneless and skinless, cut into
   1-inch cubes

*I*n a large bowl combine garlic, ginger, wine, vinegar, soy, sesame oil, vegetable oil, and sherry. Blend well. Add chicken cubes. Cover bowl with plastic wrap and marinate in refrigerator about 3 hours.

Skewer chicken pieces together. If serving as an appetizer or hors d'oeuvre, use small skewers with about 5 or 6 pieces of chicken on each.

Prepare grill. When heat is medium-high add chicken. Cook chicken about 7 to 10 minutes, turning frequently until meat is golden brown and juices run clear. Garnish with flowering kale or savoy cabbage.

Makes 1 1/2 cups marinade
Makes 4 to 6 skewers of about 5 pieces of chicken each
Serves 4 to 6

SESAME

SWORDFISH

KEBOBS

PERFECT TIMING

The Day Before:
Make fruit salad. Clean snowpeas. Grate ginger for peas. Make marinade for chicken and swordfish; refrigerate.

The Day Of:
3 hours before ready to grill, marinate chicken. 2 hours before ready to grill, marinate swordfish. 10 minutes before preparing grill, start rice. When done, remove from heat and keep covered. Soak wooden skewers. Prepare grill. When grill is hot, cook chicken. Keep warm in oven. Scrape down grill well with wire brush. Grill swordfish. 5 minutes before done sauté snowpeas.

1 heaping teaspoon Dijon-style mustard
2 large cloves garlic, minced
2 tablespoons low sodium soy sauce
1/4 teaspoon hot red pepper flakes
2 tablespoons white wine vinegar
3 tablespoons sesame oil
1/4 cup corn oil
1 teaspoon honey
2 1/2 pounds swordfish steak, cut into 2-inch
    cubes

*I*n a medium-sized bowl, combine mustard, garlic, soy, red pepper flakes, vinegar, sesame oil, corn oil, and honey. Blend well with wire whisk. Add swordfish and toss to coat well. Cover bowl with plastic wrap and marinate in refrigerator for 2 hours.

Prepare grill. Skewer swordfish making sure that the pieces are not touching each other. Grill over high heat about 5 to 7 minutes, turning frequently, until flesh is juicy and just opaque. Do not overcook since this will make the fish very dry.

To serve, place rice in center of each plate. Unskewer the swordfish, keeping in its kebob shape, over the rice. Fan snow peas at top of plate.

Makes about 3/4 cup marinade
Serves 4

Grilled Marinated Pepper Appetizer

Boneless Loin Lamb Chop with Port Wine Sauce

Pommes Purée with Herbs de Provence

Sautéed Whole Shallots

Chocolate Genoise with Grand Marnier Whipped Cream

Wine: Nuits Saint George

GRILLED MARINATED PEPPER APPETIZER

2 red bell peppers
2 yellow bell peppers
2 green bell peppers
¼ cup extra virgin olive oil
2 small cloves garlic, crushed
2 tablespoons chopped fresh basil
¼ teaspoon salt
freshly ground black pepper, to taste
2 tablespoons Balsamic vinegar
½ pound parmesan cheese, in one chunk

Prepare grill. Coat all the peppers with a little of the olive oil. While heat is very hot, place peppers on grill and char, turning until black on all sides, 5 to 10 minutes. Remove peppers from grill and place in paper bag or in covered bowl to steam for about 5 minutes. Peel peppers, then cut in half and remove all seeds and white pith. Cut each pepper half into julienne strips and place in medium-size mixing bowl. Add remaining olive oil and toss to coat. Add garlic, basil, salt, and black pepper and toss. Add Balsamic vinegar and toss. Let sit at room temperature for 1 hour before serving. Divide the peppers evenly between 4 to 6 plates. With a vegetable peeler or sharp knife shave pieces of parmesan over the peppers, or shave the cheese into a separate bowl to pass and let your guests help themselves. Serve with crusty Italian peasant bread.

Serves 4 to 6

BONELESS LOIN

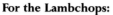

LAMBCHOPS WITH

PORT WINE SAUCE

PERFECT TIMING

The Day Before:
Grill and marinate peppers up to two days in advance. Bake chocolate genoise.

For the Lambchops:
4 to 6 double thick loin lambchops, about 1½
    to 2 inches thick

For the Sauce:
1 tablespoon sweet butter
¼ cup leeks, thinly sliced
2 tablespoons onion, finely chopped
2 large shallots, minced
½ cup chicken stock or broth
1 branch fresh thyme
¼ cup Port wine
salt and black pepper, to taste

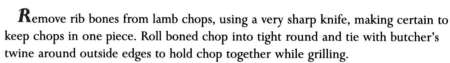

Remove rib bones from lamb chops, using a very sharp knife, making certain to keep chops in one piece. Roll boned chop into tight round and tie with butcher's twine around outside edges to hold chop together while grilling.

    Prepare the grill. While heat is very hot, sear chops for 2 to 3 minutes on each side. Remove chops until heat is medium then continue slower cooking. Cover with grill lid or with foil tent. Cook for about 7 to 10 minutes on each side or until desired doneness.

    While chops are grilling, make sauce. In a small saucepan, over high heat, add butter. When butter is hot, add leeks and onion. Sauté 1 to 2 minutes, stirring constantly, until softened. Add shallots and continue to cook, stirring, about 30 seconds.

© E. Alan McGee/FPG International

The Day Of:

Make Grand Marnier whipped cream about 1 hour before ready to grill, keep refrigerated. Peel shallots. Make the Port wine sauce while the lamb is grilling or up to 30 minutes before cooking the lamb. Keep it warm in a double boiler, or reheat it 3 minutes before ready to serve lamb. 25 minutes before you're ready to grill the lamb, boil peeled, chunked potatoes. When done, remove from heat, drain, keep covered and in a warm place. Blanch whole shallots for 5 minutes in salted, boiling water. Drain and reserve. Prepare grill. Mash potatoes and keep warm in oven. Or try piping them onto the plate through a pastry bag fitted with a star-shaped tip. Grill lamb. 5 minutes before lamb is ready to be served, sauté shallots until tender.

Add chicken stock. Bring to a boil, add thyme, and reduce heat to medium. Simmer about 15 minutes. Add Port wine and continue to simmer for 5 minutes. Remove from heat. Strain through a fine sieve. Season with salt and pepper to taste and keep warm. Sauce should be the consistency of an *au jus*.

To serve, remove cooked lamb to cutting board and allow to sit about 10 minutes. Remove butcher's twine and thinly slice. Spoon sauce over lamb.

Serves 4 to 6

© Emily Johnson/Envision

- *Grilled Wild Mushrooms*

- *Fireside Quail*

Salsify or Baby Turnips

Couscous

Assorted Fruit Tartlets

Wine: Robert Mondavi Chardonnay

¹/₂ cup extra virgin olive oil
4 large cloves garlic, crushed
1 tablespoon chopped fresh thyme leaves
2 pounds assorted wild mushrooms, such as
    shitake, oyster, porcini, and cremini
¹/₄ cup finely chopped fresh parsley
salt and freshly ground black pepper, to taste

*I*n a large bowl, combine olive oil, garlic, thyme, and mushrooms. Toss to coat thoroughly. Let it sit for 1 hour.

Prepare grill. When heat is medium-high, add mushrooms. Cook 2 to 3 minutes, turning, or until golden and tender. Remove and sprinkle with chopped parsley and season with salt and pepper. Divide mushrooms evenly between 4 to 6 appetizer plates and serve with crusty french bread.

Serves 4 to 6

NOTE: This dish can also be served as a vegetable accompaniment to many entrees.

FIRESIDE QUAIL

PERFECT TIMING

The Day Before:
Make fruit tartlets. Marinate quail. Pare and trim salsify or baby turnips.

The Day Of:
Marinate mushrooms. Prepare grill. Grill mushrooms and serve. Bring a pot of salted water or chicken broth to boil for salsify or turnips and put another one on for couscous. Start to grill quail when water boils. When quail has about 10 minutes until done, add salsify to water, cook until tender. When quail is turned to second side, cook couscous, remove from heat, keep covered.

4 tablespoons whole grain mustard
2 tablespoons cider vinegar
4 large shallots, minced
2 tablespoons honey
1 medium yellow onion, finely chopped
¼ cup dry white wine
1 teaspoon chopped fresh thyme leaves
12 quails, split with breast bone removed
36 pieces of salsify or 24 turnip slices
1 bunch watercress

*I*n a large bowl combine mustard, vinegar, shallots, honey, onion, wine, and thyme. Blend thoroughly. Add quail. Toss to coat. Let marinate in refrigerator overnight.

Prepare grill. When heat is medium-high, place quail on grill and grill about 10 to 15 minutes on each side or until juices run clear.

To serve, make a small pile of couscous in the center of each plate. Arrange two quails with breast sides up against the mound of couscous. Place 3 pieces of salsify or 2 turnip slices on each side of mounded couscous and quails, and garnish each plate with a bunch of watercress.

Makes 1 cup marinade
Serves 6

Watercress and Enoki Mushroom Salad with Lemon Vinaigrette

■ *Japanese Marinated Grilled Tuna Steak*

■ *Grilled Red Onion Slices*

Steamed Baby Patty Pan Squash

Tangerine Mousse

Wine: Verdicchio

JAPANESE MARINATED GRILLED TUNA STEAK

© Steven Mark Needham/Envision

1 3-inch piece fresh ginger, peeled and grated
3 large cloves garlic, minced
1 teaspoon honey
1/2 cup Mirin wine
2 tablespoons low sodium soy sauce
1/4 teaspoon hot chili oil
1/2 cup vegetable oil
6 6-ounce tuna steaks, about 1/2 to 1-inch thick

In a shallow glass dish, combine ginger, garlic, honey, wine, soy, chili oil, and vegetable oil. Whisk to blend well. Lay the tuna steaks side by side in the dish and toss to coat. Cover dish with plastic wrap and refrigerate 3 to 4 hours.

Prepare grill. When heat is medium-high, add steaks to grill. Do not crowd them together. Cook 3 to 5 minutes per side or until desired doneness. Ideally, the flesh should be slightly pink in the center.

Makes about 3/4 cup marinade
Serves 6

GRILLED RED

ONION SLICES

PERFECT TIMING

The Day Before:
Make the tangerine mousse and refrigerate. Make both the lemon vinaigrette and the tuna marinade.

The Day Of:
3 to 4 hours before you are ready to grill, marinate tuna. Make salad and refrigerate. Slice red onions. Prepare grill. Grill tuna steaks and put water on to boil the squash. Remove tuna from grill and keep warm in oven while grilling onions. When you add onions to grill, cook squash. Both the onions and the squash should be ready about the same time.

3 to 4 medium-sized red onions, peeled and cut
    into ¹/₂-inch thick slices
¹/₄ cup extra virgin olive oil
¹/₂ teaspoon salt
freshly ground black pepper, to taste

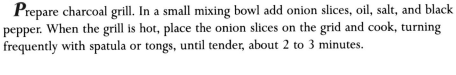

*P*repare charcoal grill. In a small mixing bowl add onion slices, oil, salt, and black pepper. When the grill is hot, place the onion slices on the grid and cook, turning frequently with spatula or tongs, until tender, about 2 to 3 minutes.

Serves 6

Grilled Vietnamese Pork Salad

Cold Sesame Noodles

Lemon Shrimp

Stir-Fried Mixed Vegetables with Toasted Sesame Seeds

Pineapple

Chinese Black Tea

Tsing Tao Beer

GRILLED

VIETNAMESE PORK

SALAD WITH

MINT AND CHILE

DRESSING

© John Dominis/Wheeler Pictures

½ pound boneless pork shoulder, trimmed of
    excess fat
3 large cloves garlic, minced
2 tablespoons low sodium soy sauce
1 tablespoon vegetable oil
1 medium onion, thinly sliced
1 ½ tablespoons cider vinegar
2 tablespoons freshly squeezed lime juice
¼ cup chopped mint plus 2 tablespoons
    julienned mint
¼ hot chile pepper, seeded and chopped
¼ teaspoon Szechuan hot bean paste
½ teaspoon sugar
¼ teaspoon salt
2 large white turnips, peeled
2 large carrots, peeled
3 cups thinly sliced Romaine lettuce leaves
    (about 1 large head)
3 cups thinly sliced Savoy cabbage (about 1
    small head)
½ cup unsalted peanuts, coarsely chopped

Although this salad may seem a little intimidating in terms of the number of ingredients it requires, a lot of the preparation can be done the day before.

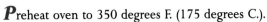

Preheat oven to 350 degrees F. (175 degrees C.).

In a medium bowl, toss pork with garlic and soy sauce. Set aside to marinate at room temperature for about 1 hour.

In a medium-sized, oven-proof skillet, over medium-high heat, add 2 teaspoons of the vegetable oil. Add the onion slices and cook, stirring occasionally, until the onions are evenly browned, about 5 minutes. Place the skillet in the oven and cook, stirring occasionally until the onions are dry and deep brown, about 25 minutes. Remove onions from skillet and set aside.

In a medium bowl, whisk the vinegar, lime juice, chopped mint, hot chile pepper, bean paste, sugar, salt, and ⅓ cup water to blend. Set the dressing aside.

Using a food processor fitted with a grating disk, or a hand held grater, shred the turnips. Place them in a bowl and toss them with 3 tablespoons of the dressing. Shred the carrots and place them in another bowl and toss with 3 tablespoons of the dressing.

Prepare grill. Grill pork over high heat for about 10 to 15 minutes on each side or until desired doneness. Remove to warm platter and allow to sit for about 10 minutes. Cut pork into ¼-inch (½-centimeter) thick strips. Set aside to cool further.

In a large bowl, toss the lettuce, cabbage, julienned mint, pork, and remaining dressing. Arrange the turnips and carrots on opposite sides of 4 to 6 salad plates and place the pork and salad mixture in the center. Sprinkle with the charred onions and chopped peanuts.

Makes ½ cup dressing
Serves 4 to 6

LEMON SHRIMP

3 large cloves garlic, minced
1 2-inch piece peeled and grated fresh ginger
2 teaspoons Dijon-style mustard
1 teaspoon hot red pepper flakes
1 hot chile pepper, seeded and roughly chopped
½ to 1 teaspoon salt
1 tablespoon chopped lemon grass (optional)
¼ cup freshly squeezed lemon juice
¼ cup extra virgin olive oil
1½ pounds large shrimp

*I*n a large glass bowl, combine garlic, ginger, mustard, hot red pepper flakes, chile pepper, salt, lemon grass, and lemon juice. In a thin stream, slowly whisk in olive oil until well blended. Set aside.

Devein shrimp by cutting along top edge with sharp knife or scissors. Remove feet but keep the shell intact. Rinse under cold water, then pat dry with paper towel. Add cleaned shrimp to marinade. Toss to coat. Cover bowl with plastic wrap and refrigerate for about 3 hours.

Prepare grill. Grill shrimp over medium-high heat for about 5 to 10 minutes depending on desired doneness. Do not overcook or shrimp will become tough. Serve with plenty of fresh lemon wedges.

Makes about ¾ cup marinade
Serves 4 to 6

PERFECT TIMING

The Day Before:
Grate carrots and turnips. Store in separate resealable plastic bags in refrigerator. Slice cabbage and romaine lettuce and store in resealable plastic bag in refrigerator. Chop mint and peanuts. Make sesame sauce for noodles and refrigerate. Make noodles and store in refrigerator. Peel garlic and ginger. Make dressing for pork. Make marinade for shrimp. Refrigerate. Clean shrimp. Refrigerate until ready to add to marinade. Char onions, cool, and place in resealable plastic bag. Toast sesame seeds for the vegetable

stir-fry. Cut up assorted vegetables for stir-fry and keep in separate plastic bags until ready to sauté. Remember that when you start to sauté your vegetables, begin with the ones that take the longest to cook, such as carrots, and finish with the ones that take the least time to cook, such as zucchini and snow peas.

The Day Of:

Marinate shrimp 3 hours before you are ready to grill and the pork 1 hour before. Combine noodles with sesame sauce just before serving. Prepare grill. Grill pork. Remove pork when cooked. Scrape down grill and assemble salad. Serve salad with the sesame noodles.

Savoy Cabbage Salad with Soy Vinaigrette

■ *Grilled Soft Shelled Crabs with Ginger and Black Beans*

Stir-Fried Julienned Leeks

Garlic-Herb Bread

Carrot Cake

Wine: Domaine Chandon "Blanc de Noir"

GRILLED SOFT SHELL CRABS WITH GINGER AND BLACK BEANS

8 jumbo soft shell crabs, cleaned
1/4 cup vegetable oil
1 teaspoon sesame oil
2 large cloves garlic, crushed
1 2-inch piece fresh ginger, peeled and grated
2 tablespoons salted, fermented black beans, rinsed well and drained*
1 tablespoon freshly squeezed lemon juice
1 bunch scallions, minced
cayenne pepper, to taste
salt and freshly ground black pepper to taste
seaweed (optional)**

*H*ave the crabs cleaned at the fish market when you buy them. Keep refrigerated until ready to grill.

In a medium-sized sauté pan, over high heat, add both vegetable oil and sesame oil. When hot, add garlic and ginger, stirring constantly for 1 to 2 minutes. Add black beans and stir until heated through, about 1 minute. Stir in lemon juice and minced scallions and cook an additional 2 to 3 minutes. Season to taste with cayenne pepper. Remove from heat and keep warm while grilling crabs.

Prepare charcoal grill. When heat is medium hot, brush both sides of crabs with a little olive oil and season with salt and freshly ground black pepper. Grill approximately 3 to 4 minutes on each side, until nicely crisp and deep reddish brown.

Perfect Timing

The Day Before:
Thinly slice the cabbage, then blanch in boiling water, drain, and chill. Make soy vinaigrette and refrigerate. Two hours before serving, toss cabbage with vinaigrette. It should be allowed to marinate for two hours before serving. Pare and grate ginger. Peel garlic. Julienne leeks. Wash well. Drain and store in resealable plastic bag in refrigerator. Make garlic-herb butter. Make carrot cake.

© Sandy Roessler/FPG International

The Day Of:
Butter french bread baguette with garlic-herb butter and wrap tightly in aluminum foil. Prepare grill. 15 to 20 minutes before you are ready to grill crabs, make sauce and keep in pan to reheat. Place crabs on grill, and start to sauté leeks. 4 minutes before crabs are done, put bread in preheated 350 degree F. (175 degree C.) oven. Remove leeks to oven-proof platter and keep warm in oven, if necessary. Two minutes before crabs are done, heat sauce over medium heat. Remove crabs from grill. Remove bread from oven.

To serve, arrange two crabs on top of seaweed, if desired, and drizzle a little bit of the sauce over both (about 1 tablespoon per plate).

Blanch seaweed in boiling water for one minute until it is a beautiful bright green. Arrange a small amount in the center of each plate. Make a rim of sautéed leeks around the crabs and seaweed.

Makes about ½ cup sauce
Serves 4

* Fermented black beans are widely available in oriental markets and in supermarkets. China Bowl brand is the best that I have found.

** Order seaweed from your local fish market.

Miniature Eggrolls with Horseradish Mustard

■ *Grilled Pork Tenderloin in Black Soy and Rock Candy Marinade*

Sautéed Bok Choy, Carrots, and Bean Sprouts

Steamed Oriental-Style Short Grain Rice

Almond Cookies and Orange Sections

Green Tea

Kirin Beer

GRILLED PORK TENDERLOIN IN BLACK SOY AND ROCK CANDY MARINADE

1 tablespoon vegetable oil
2 large shallots, minced
4 large cloves garlic, crushed
1 2-inch piece fresh ginger, peeled and sliced
    into 1/8-inch slices
4 scallions, trimmed and thinly sliced
1/4 cup Mirin wine
1/4 cup black soy sauce*
4 ounces rock candy or 2 ounces turbinado
    sugar
2 star anise*
1 cup water
2 tablespoons Oriental sesame oil
2 pounds pork tenderloin, in one or two pieces

*I*n a 2-quart (2-liter) saucepan over high heat, add vegetable oil. When oil is hot, add shallots, stirring constantly, about 30 seconds. Add garlic, ginger, and scallions. Stir constantly until wilted, about 2 minutes. Add wine, soy sauce, rock candy or sugar, star anise, and water. Bring to boil. Reduce heat to medium and simmer 15 to 20 minutes, stirring occasionally. Remove from heat, stir in sesame oil and cool to room temperature. When cooled completely pour over pork tenderloin, cover and let

Ralph B. Pleasant/FPG International

Make the eggrolls up to a week in advance and store them in the freezer until ready to fry.

The Day Before:
Make horseradish mustard. Marinate the pork tenderloin. Cut bok choy and carrots.

The Day Of:
Prepare grill. Heat oil and fry eggrolls. Drain on paper towel and keep warm in oven. Place pork on grill and start to cook rice, both of which should only take about 20 minutes. 10 minutes before rice and pork are done, begin to sauté Oriental vegetables.

marinate in refrigerator 6 hours or overnight.

Prepare grill. When heat is medium-high, place pork on grill. Cook, covered, 15 to 20 minutes or until desired doneness, turning occasionally. Remove pork to cutting board and slice into ¼-inch to ½-inch (½ centimeter to 1 centimeter) pieces. Lay meat slices down the center of a serving platter. Spoon marinade over top of meat. Arrange vegetables on either side of the pork.

Makes about 1½ cups marinade
Serves 6 to 8

*Black soy sauce and star anise are available in Oriental markets, as well as many supermarkets.

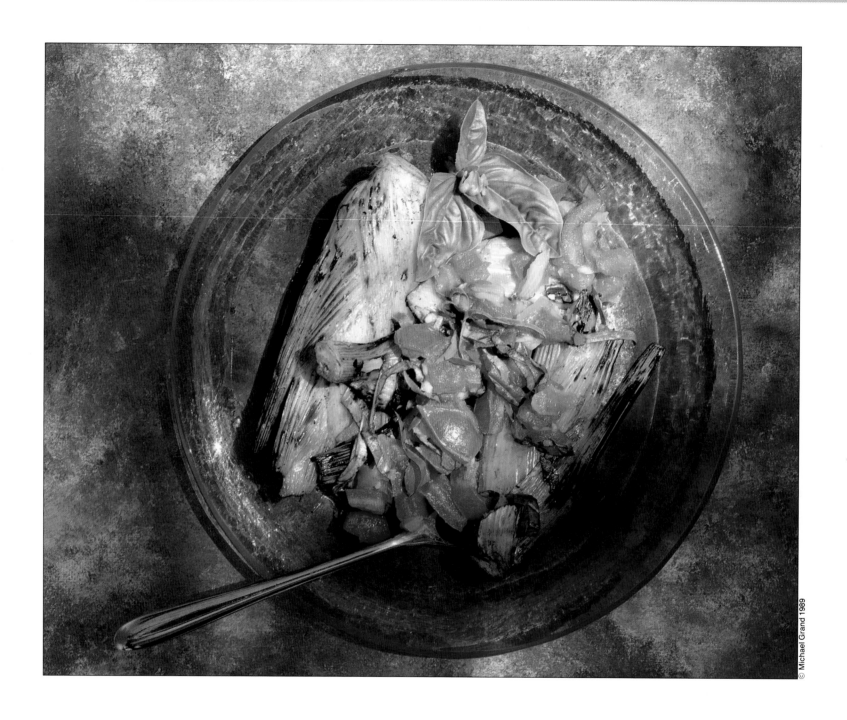

© Michael Grand 1989

Grilled Fennel with Tomato, Basil, and Garlic

▪ Charcoal Grilled Lobster with Coral and Tamale Vinaigrette

Fresh Corn and Bell Pepper Salad

Oven Baked Sweet Potato Chips

Blueberry Crisp

Wine: Saint Veran

GRILLED FENNEL WITH TOMATO, BASIL, AND GARLIC

PERFECT TIMING

The Day Before:
Make the tomato-basil sauce up to a day in advance so all that has to be done is grill the fennel and reheat the sauce. Make corn and bell pepper salad.

4 fennel bulbs, trimmed
1/4 cup plus 2 tablespoons extra virgin olive oil
1/4 cup minced onions
2 large cloves garlic, chopped
5 large ripe plum tomatoes, seeded and diced
1 tablespoon freshly squeezed lemon juice
2 tablespoons chopped basil plus 12 leaves
    for garnish
salt and freshly ground black pepper, to taste

*P*repare grill. Cut fennel into 1/4-inch (1/2 centimeter) slices. Brush both sides generously with olive oil and season with salt and black pepper to taste. When heat is high, add fennel slices and cook, covered, for 3 to 5 minutes on each side or until tender when pierced with a knife. Remove to platter and keep warm in oven.

In 8-inch skillet, heat 2 tablespoons of olive oil over high heat. When hot, add onions and cook, stirring constantly for 1 to 2 minutes or until transparent. Add garlic and cook, stirring, about 30 seconds. Add chopped tomato and lemon juice. Continue cooking about 3 minutes. Remove from heat. Stir in chopped basil and season with salt and plenty of freshly ground black pepper to taste.

To serve, overlap 2 slices of fennel and spoon about 1 tablespoon tomato-basil sauce over middle. Garnish with fresh basil leaves.

Serves 6

GREAT
GRILLING

CHARCOAL GRILLED LOBSTER WITH CORAL AND TAMALE VINAIGRETTE

6 1-1½ pound live lobsters
1 tablespoon coarse sea salt
2 teaspoons truffle or Dijon-style mustard
1 small clove garlic, minced
¼ cup white wine vinegar
½ cup salad oil
freshly ground black pepper, to taste
2 tablespoons freshly chopped parsley

The Day Of:
Bake the blueberry crisp and let it sit at room temperature. Have all the ingredients ready to make the coral vinaigrette except for the coral and tamale. Prepare grill. Bake sweet potato chips. When grill is ready, cook fennel. When you turn fennel to the second side slowly heat up the basil sauce. Serve fennel. Warm platter in oven for lobsters. Grill lobsters. Remove from heat. Cut out coral and tamale and reserve. Keep lobsters warm in oven while making vinaigrette.

*T*o prepare lobsters for the grill, bring 10 to 12 quarts (9 to 11 liters) salted water to a rapid boil. Plunge the lobsters, head first, into the boiling water for 1 minute. Drain.

Prepare a low wood charcoal fire and put lobsters on grid. Cook 10 to 12 minutes, turning frequently. Remove the lobsters, let them cool slightly, then cut them in half lengthwise through center of head and tail and remove the coral and tamale.*
Reserve coral and tamale and keep lobsters warm in oven while making vinaigrette.

In the bowl of a food processor fitted with a steel blade, combine reserved coral, tamale, truffle or Dijon mustard, garlic, and wine vinegar. With processor running, slowly add oil in thin stream and whisk until emulsified. Season with salt, pepper, and chopped parsley. Drizzle dressing over lobster or serve in separate small ramekins. Makes about 1 cup dressing.

Serves 6

*The coral of the lobster is the reddish ovary; the tamale is the greenish part of the roe.

Artichokes Vinaigrette

■*Grilled Boneless Leg of Lamb with Chiles and Mint*

Parmesan Broiled Tomatoes

Chocolate Truffle Cake with Mocha Buttercream

Espresso

Wine: Chianti Classico

GRILLED BONELESS LEG OF LAMB WITH CHILES AND MINT

1 small head of garlic
5 small chili peppers, seeded and roughly chopped
½ cup freshly squeezed lemon juice
1 heaping tablespoon grain mustard
2 teaspoons hot chili paste with garlic
1 bunch fresh mint
1 3-pound boned leg of lamb, trimmed of fat, rolled, and tied

PERFECT TIMING

The Day Before:
Make cake and ice with butter-cream frosting. Refrigerate. Cook artichokes and chill. Make vinaigrette. Chill. Marinate lamb.

© Susanna Pashko/Envision

*I*n the bowl of a food processor fitted with a steel blade, combine garlic, chiles, lemon juice, mustard, chili paste, and mint. Process until mixture is fairly smooth. Spread mixture over entire roast and allow to marinate overnight. Turn periodically during this time to ensure even marination.

Prepare grill. Over high heat, sear roast on all sides to seal in juices. Remove roast until heat reduces to medium-high. Return lamb to grill, cover and cook, turning occasionally, about 30 minutes or until desired doneness. Remove lamb to cutting board and allow it to sit about 10 to 15 minutes before slicing.

To serve, place slices on a large platter, sprinkled with more fresh mint and surrounded by broiled tomatoes.

Serves 8 to 10

© Susanna Pashko/Envision

The Day Of:
*Prepare grill. Grill lamb.
Cut tomatoes in half. Twenty
minutes before lamb is done,
turn on oven broiler. Grate parmesan cheese over tops of tomatoes, drizzle with a little olive
oil, and season with freshly
ground black pepper. Broil until
tender, about 5 to 7 minutes.*

*To serve the artichokes, remove
leaves and hollow out center and
remove hairlike fibers attached
to the heart. Arrange leaves in
circle around artichoke's heart
so it will look like an open
flower. Serve the vinaigrette in
tiny glass ramekins on the side.*

*Baked Goat Cheese
Croustades*

▪ *Grilled Veal Chops
with Peach and
Apricot Chutney*

▪ *Grilled Mixed
Baby Vegetables*

*Roasted
Potato Wedges*

*Open-Faced
Apple Pie*

*Wine:
Sterling Vineyards
Cabernet Sauvignon*

GRILLED VEAL CHOPS WITH PEACH AND APRICOT CHUTNEY

© Michael Grand 1989

For the Peach and Apricot Chutney
2 large peaches, peeled and chopped
1 cup chopped dried apricots
1 medium onion, coarsely chopped
1/2 cup dark raisins
1/2 cup honey
1/2 cup cider vinegar
1/4 cup freshly squeezed orange juice
1/2 cup fresh lemon juice
1 3-inch piece ginger, peeled and chopped
3 large cloves garlic, crushed
1 cinnamon stick
1 teaspoon dried mustard
1/2 teaspoon ground allspice
1/4 teaspoon ground cloves
1 teaspoon hot red pepper flakes

*I*n a heavy gauge 3-quart (3-liter) saucepan, over high heat, combine all of the above ingredients. Bring to boil. Reduce heat to low and simmer until thickened to chutney consistency, stirring occasionally, about 35 to 40 minutes. Transfer chutney to bowl and allow to cool at room temperature. Cover with plastic wrap and refrigerate overnight. Remove from refrigerator at least 2 hours before using so that it has enough time to reach room temperature.

© Michael Grand 1989

For the Grilled Veal Chops
4 to 8 loin veal chops, about 1 to 2 inches thick
extra virgin olive oil
salt and freshly ground black pepper, to taste
2 to 3 peaches halved, pitted, and peeled

Prepare grill. Brush each side of veal chops with olive oil and season with salt and black pepper to taste. Sear chops over high heat for 2 to 3 minutes. Then make a quarter turn, and sear another 2 to 3 minutes. Remove from grill until heat is medium high. Grill chops about 7 to 10 minutes more on each side or until desired doneness. Chops should be slightly pink in center. Serve with the chutney spooned over peach halves.

Makes about 3 cups chutney
Serves 4 to 6

G R I L L E D

M I X E D

B A B Y

V E G E T A B L E S

8 baby eggplant
8 baby zucchini
8 pearl onions, peeled
8 baby patty pan squash
8 small white mushrooms
1 large red bell pepper, cut into 8 squares
extra virgin olive oil
salt and freshly ground black pepper

*W*ash the vegetables. Generously coat them with the olive oil. Season with salt and pepper.

Prepare grill. Soak about 12 to 14 wooden skewers in warm water for about 30 minutes. Skewer the vegetables so that they will lie as flat as possible on the grill depending on their natural shape. Grill over medium-high heat about 7 to 10 minutes or until tender when pierced with a knife; some vegetables will be done more quickly than others, depending on size and shape.

Serves 4

PERFECT TIMING

Make the chutney up to two weeks in advance; keep refrigerated until 2 hours before ready to use, and let warm to room temperature.

The Day Before:
Toast French bread for croustades. Make apple pie and leave it out at room temperature. Clean and cut up mixed vegetables.

The Day Of:
Prepare potatoes, cover and reserve. Soak wooden skewers in warm water at least 30 minutes before them, if necessary. Bake goat cheese croustades. Prepare grill. At the same time, start to roast potato wedges. Skewer mixed vegetables. Grill vegetables. Keep warm in oven. Grill veal chops. Potatoes should be ready when you remove veal chops from the grill.

GREAT
GRILLING

Vegetable Paté with Watercress Mayonnaise

- *Swordfish Grilled over Citrus Peel with Blood Orange Butter Sauce*

Sauté of Julienne Carrots and Zucchini Squash

Fresh Sliced Papaya on Mango Purée

Wine: Sylvaner

SWORDFISH GRILLED OVER CITRUS PEELS WITH BLOOD ORANGE BUTTER SAUCE

PERFECT TIMING

Make vegetable paté up to two days in advance and the mayonnaise up to a day before.

The Day Before:
Julienne carrots and zucchini. Store separately in refrigerator in resealable plastic bags. Purée mangoes, add a little lemon juice to keep color. Cover and refrigerate.

For the Swordfish
6 6-ounce swordfish steaks, about 1 to 1½-
   inches thick
salt and freshly ground black pepper, to taste
1 cup dried citrus peels, soaked in warm water
   for about 30 minutes

Prepare the grill. When grill is hot, remove grid using heat proof mitts or gloves. Sprinkle citrus peelings over coals or lava rocks. Replace grid and allow it to get hot again, about 2 minutes. Brush grid with oil. Season swordfish with salt and pepper. Place swordfish on grill, cover, and cook about 5 minutes on each side or until flesh flakes easily.

© Michael Grand 1989

GREAT
GRILLING

For the Sauce
½ cup dry white wine
3 large shallots, minced
½ pound sweet butter, softened to room
    temperature
¼ cup blood orange juice
salt and white pepper, to taste

The Day Of:
Prepare grill. Make blood orange sauce up to 30 minutes ahead and keep warm in double boiler or reheat 3 minutes before fish is done.
Grill swordfish. When you turn swordfish to cook second side, start to sauté the julienne vegetables. Remove from heat when tender but still al dente. Vegetables should be ready when fish is done and vice versa but keep vegetables warm in oven if fish needs to cook a bit more.

*I*n a small saucepan over high heat, combine white wine and shallots. Bring to boil and allow liquid to evaporate until almost dry. With a wire whisk, slowly whip in butter until it has completely melted. Bring to boil and remove from heat. Stir in orange juice and season with salt and white pepper to taste. Makes about 1 cup sauce.

For the Garnish
1 blood orange, sliced into 12 paper thin rounds
½ cup water
¼ cup granulated sugar

*I*n a 1-quart (1-liter) saucepan over high heat, combine water and sugar. Bring to boil and cook, stirring occasionally, 3 to 5 minutes until mixture is a light syrupy consistency. Remove from heat, add orange slices and let sit in liquid for about 2 to 3 minutes. Remove orange slices to wax paper until ready to use.

  To serve: spoon about 2 tablespoons blood orange sauce on the bottom of each dinner plate. Place a border of vegetables around the rim of the plate. Place grilled swordfish in center, and top it with two pieces of overlapping blood orange rounds on top.

Serves 6

© Michael Grand 1989

GREAT
GRILLING

Summer Tomatoes with Fresh Mozzarella, Basil, and Extra Virgin Olive Oil

▪ Grilled Chicken with Sundried Tomatoes, Garlic, and Fusilli Pasta

Sourdough Baguettes

Amaretti Cookies

Espresso

Wine: Valpolicella

GRILLED CHICKEN WITH SUNDRIED TOMATOES, GARLIC, AND FUSILLI PASTA

4 tablespoons extra virgin olive oil
2 whole chicken breasts, boneless and skinless
1 pound fusilli pasta
1 cup dried and unsalted sundried tomatoes,
    softened in hot water for 10 to 15 minutes
    and julienned*
3 small cloves garlic, minced
¼ cup chopped Italian parsley
salt and freshly ground black pepper, to taste

Brush chicken breasts with about 2 tablespoons of the olive oil. Season with salt and black pepper to taste. Prepare grill. When heat is high, add chicken breasts. Cover and cook about 10 to 15 minutes on each side or until done.

While chicken is grilling, bring 3 quarts (3 liters) salted water to boil over high heat. Add pasta. Stir until water boils again. Cook 5 to 7 minutes or until pasta is *al dente*. Drain pasta in colander. Drizzle with 1 tablespoon olive oil and toss.

Remove chicken from grill. Keep warm on platter covered with aluminum foil or in warm oven.

© R. Chandler/FPG International

The Day Before:
Cover and refrigerate. Soak sun-dried tomatoes in warm water. Chop parsley. Place in resealable plastic bag.

The Day Of:
Cook pasta, drain, and rinse gently under cold water. Chop garlic. Slice tomatoes. Slice mozzarella. Julienne basil leaves.

In small sauté pan over medium-high heat, add remaining 1 tablespoon olive oil. When hot, add garlic and stir 1 to 2 minutes. Add sundried tomatoes and cook, stirring, 1 to 2 minutes until heated through. Remove from heat. Add to pasta, then add chopped parsley and toss. Shred chicken into thin strips. Add to pasta and toss. Season with salt and plenty of freshly ground black pepper.

Serves 4 to 6

*Sundried tomatoes come in many forms. The most popular are those packed in olive oil. I prefer the dried tomatoes, which must be reconstituted in water. These also come in two forms—dried and salted, and dried and unsalted. For this recipe I used dried and unsalted tomatoes, which allowed me to have some control over how much salt and oil I used. However, buy different types to see which ones you prefer.

- *Grilled Leeks Vinaigrette*

- *Herb-Grilled Trout*

Sautéed Cherry Tomatoes with Olive Oil and Sliced Garlic

Pommes Anna Crème Brûlée

Wine: Premier Cru Chablis

16 small to medium leeks
extra virgin olive oil

*I*n a large pot, bring 3 quarts (3-liters) of salted water to boil over high heat. Trim root ends and about 4 inches of green tops of the leeks. Slit each leek lengthwise to within ¹/₂-inch of root end, leaving them whole. Rinse leeks well under cold water. Using butcher's twine, tie leeks together in four bunches of four. Blanch them in the boiling water until just tender, about 5 to 7 minutes. Drain and rinse under cold water. Untie leeks and pat dry with paper towels.

Prepare grill. Brush leeks with extra virgin olive oil. Grill leeks over medium-high heat, in two batches if grill is small, and cook 7 to 10 minutes, turning frequently, until leeks are nicely charred. Remove first batch and keep in oven until finished grilling second batch.

For the Vinaigrette
2 tablespoons dried mustard
1 teaspoon chopped fresh thyme
2 teaspoons chopped fresh basil
2 tablespoons balsamic vinegar
¹/₂ cup extra virgin olive oil
1 hard boiled egg, chopped
salt and freshly ground black pepper, to taste
2 tablespoons chopped fresh parsley

*I*n a small mixing bowl, combine mustard, thyme, basil, and vinegar. Use a wire whisk to blend ingredients together. Slowly whisk in olive oil in a thin stream, until it emulsifies. Stir in chopped egg and season with salt and pepper, to taste.

To serve, place 4 leeks on each of four appetizer plates with the tops all pointed the same direction. Drizzle dressing over leeks and sprinkle with a little chopped parsley.

Makes about 1 cup dressing
Serves 4

HERB-GRILLED

TROUT

2 tablespoons chopped fresh marjoram
2 tablespoons chopped fresh lemon thyme or
   culinary thyme
2 tablespoons chopped fresh parsley
3 lemons
salt and ground white pepper, to taste
4 whole brook trout, with head and tail intact, cleaned

PERFECT TIMING

The Day Before:
Make crème brûlée and keep refrigerated. Make vinaigrette for leeks. Refrigerate. Blanch leeks and refrigerate. Chop herb mixture for trout. Slice garlic cloves. Peel potatoes and keep in water.

The Day Of:
Remove leeks and vinaigrette from refrigerator 2 hours before ready to grill. Prepare grill. Make pommes Anna. They should take 25 to 30 minutes to cook. 15 minutes before grilling leeks, stuff trouts with the herb mixture. Grill leeks and serve. Grill trout. When you turn trout to second side put pan on to sauté tomatoes. Sauté tomatoes with garlic about 3 to 5 minutes.

*P*repare grill. In a small bowl combine all the herbs and mix thoroughly. Using equal amounts of the herb mixture, fill the cavity of each trout. Squeeze the juice of one lemon equally among fish cavities as well. Season both the insides and outsides of the fish with salt and pepper.

Brush the grill with vegetable oil. Grill trout over medium-high heat for about 3 to 5 minutes on each side or until flesh is opaque and pulls slightly away from the bone.

Serve with plenty of fresh lemon wedges and sprinkle trout with more fresh herbs.

Serves 4

© Michael Grand 1989

GREAT
        GRILLING

Arugula, Endive, and Red Onion Salad with Mustard Vinaigrette

■ *Grilled Sea Scallops with Pecans and Tarragon Vin Blanc Sauce*

Haricots Verts

Italian Peasant Bread

Fresh Strawberries with Cassis

Wine: David Bruce Chardonnay

GRILLED SEA SCALLOPS WITH PECANS AND TARRAGON VIN BLANC SAUCE

2 pounds sea scallops
¼ cup dry white wine
¼ cup tarragon vinegar
3 large shallots, finely minced
3 black peppercorns
5-7 sprigs fresh tarragon plus 3 tablespoons
   chopped
⅓ cup heavy cream
2 cups fish stock or broth
salt and white pepper, to taste
⅓ cup toasted pecan halves

Remove tough, fibery muscle from sides of scallops. Skewer. Season with salt and white pepper. Brush with olive oil. Reserve.

Meanwhile, in a 2-quart (2-liters) saucepan, combine white wine, vinegar, shallots, peppercorns, and sprig of tarragon. Bring to boil over high heat. Allow liquid to evaporate almost completely, until dry. Do not color the shallots. Add cream. Bring to boil. Reduce to simmer and cook 2 to 3 minutes until cream is slightly thickened. Add fish stock. Bring to boil, then reduce to simmer. Cook 15 to 20 minutes. Strain sauce through fine sieve or cheesecloth into oven-proof glass container and keep warm in a water bath or double boiler.

© Michael Grand 1989

PERFECT TIMING

The Day Before:
Make the vinaigrette for the salad and refrigerate. Toast the pecans. Clean the haricots verts and the strawberries.

The Day Of:
If using wooden skewers, soak them in warm water. Skewer scallops and keep refrigerated until ready to grill. Make the sauce for the scallops as much as 30 minutes ahead, add chopped tarragon just before serving and keep warm in water-bath or double boiler. 10 minutes before grilling fish, heat pot of salted water to cook haricot verts. Grill scallops. When you turn scallops to second side, add haricot verts to boiling water and cook about 5 minutes or until tender. Drain and reserve.

Prepare grill. Skewer scallops. Brush grid with olive oil and grill scallops over high heat about 2 to 3 minutes on each side. Scallops are done when flesh is just opaque.

When scallops are done, stir chopped tarragon into sauce. Correct seasonings with salt and white pepper.

To serve, spoon about 4 tablespoons of sauce in center of each plate. Sprinkle small amount of pecans over sauce. Remove scallops from skewers and mound small amount in center of each plate. Garnish generously with fresh tarragon sprigs.

Serves 4 to 6

Hummus

Tabbouleh

■ Cumin-Marinated
Lamb Kebobs

Sautéed Kale

Lemon Tart

Coffee with
Anisette Liqueur

Wine:
Trakkia
Cabernet Sauvignon

CUMIN-MARINATED

LAMB KEBOBS

1 tablespoon ground cumin
2 teaspoons whole coriander seeds
¹/₄ teaspoon turmeric
¹/₂ teaspoon ground cinnamon
1 teaspoon ground nutmeg
2 teaspoons salt
3 large cloves garlic, crushed
¹/₃ cup dry white wine
²/₃ cup extra virgin olive oil
1 lemon, sliced into ¹/₈-inch rounds
2 pounds lean leg of lamb, trimmed, boned, and
    cut into 2-inch cubes

PERFECT TIMING

The Day Before:
Make the hummus and the tabbouleh. Marinate lamb. Trim, rinse, and dry kale. Store in resealable plastic bag in refrigerator until ready to cook. Make lemon curd. Refrigerate. Prebake tart shell and allow to cool at room temperature. Do not refrigerate.

The Day Of:
30 minutes before grilling soak wooden skewers. Prepare grill. Cut pita bread into triangles and keep in napkin lined basket. Skewer lamb. Grill lamb. 5 minutes before lamb is done, quickly sauté kale in a little olive oil and garlic.

In the bowl of a food processor fitted with a steel blade, combine cumin, coriander seed, turmeric, cinnamon, nutmeg, salt, and garlic. Process until well combined and coriander seed is chopped. With processor running, add white wine. Slowly add olive oil until well blended. Pour marinade into medium-sized glass or ceramic bowl. Add lemon slices and cubed lamb. Toss to coat. Cover bowl with plastic wrap, and place in refrigerator for 6 hours or overnight, stir once or twice during this time.

Prepare grill. Skewer lamb cubes. Grill over high heat, turning occasionally to cook evenly on all sides, about 10 to 15 minutes or until desired doneness.

To serve, place the lamb on its skewers on a platter. Let people serve themselves buffet style.

Grilled Veal Sausage, Pepper, and Mozzarella Cheese Pizza

Paillard of Chicken with Light Pesto

Sautéed Diced Yellow, Red, and Green Bell Peppers

Amaretto Cake

Cappucino

Wine: Barolo

GRILLED VEAL SAUSAGE, PEPPER, AND MOZZARELLA CHEESE PIZZA

For the Pizza Dough— for one 14-inch pizza or
    four 4-inch pizzas
1 tablespoon dry yeast
$2/3$ cup warm water
$1/4$ cup extra virgin olive oil
$1/2$ teaspoon salt
2 cups Semolina or regular all-purpose flour
olive oil to coat

*P*reheat oven to 450 degrees F. (230° C.).
  In a large mixing bowl, add yeast to warm water. Allow it to stand for 5 minutes. Stir in olive oil, salt, and flour until well-blended. On a well-floured board, knead dough until it becomes smooth and elastic, about 15 minutes. Shape dough into a round ball. Brush it with a little olive oil to coat. Put it in bowl, cover with plastic wrap, and let it rise in a cool place for 1 hour. Punch dough down, and knead for a few more minutes. Press or roll dough with rolling pin to fit into 14-inch pizza pan; or divide dough into 4 equal parts and fit into 4-inch pans. Fill with sausage and pepper mixture. Sprinkle with fresh mozzarella and parmesan cheeses. Using a pizza stone, if possible, bake for 20 minutes or until golden brown.

For the Topping
2 tablespoons extra virgin olive oil
2 large cloves garlic, minced
1 large green bell pepper, cut into strips
1 large red bell pepper, cut into strips
2 tablespoons chopped fresh marjoram
4 veal sausages
salt and pepper, to taste
8-ounces fresh mozzarella cheese, grated (about
   1 cup)
$^{1}/_{2}$ cup grated reggiano parmesan cheese

*P*repare grill.

Meanwhile, in an 8-inch (20-centimeter) skillet, over high heat, add 1 tablespoon of oil. When hot, add garlic and cook, stirring constantly for 1 minute. Add peppers. Sauté 2 to 3 minutes until peppers are brightly colored and coated with oil. Remove from heat, stir in marjoram, and reserve.

When grill is at high heat, add veal sausages and cook, turning frequently, 3 to 5 minutes or until the sausages are cooked through. Allow them to cool until you can touch them. Cut the sausages into $^{1}/_{2}$-inch (one centimeter) pieces. Combine the veal with the peppers and toss to thoroughly incorporate. Spread over large pizza or equally between individual pizzas. Sprinkle generously with mozzarella cheese and parmesan and bake as directed.

Serves 4

PAILLARD OF CHICKEN WITH LIGHT PESTO

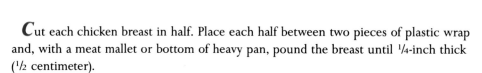

4 whole boneless, skinless chicken breasts
¼ cup extra virgin olive oil
salt and freshly ground black pepper, to taste

*C*ut each chicken breast in half. Place each half between two pieces of plastic wrap and, with a meat mallet or bottom of heavy pan, pound the breast until ¼-inch thick (½ centimeter).

Prepare grill. Remove plastic wrap from breast halves. Coat with the olive oil. Season breasts with salt and pepper. Grill breast halves over high heat for about 3 to 5 minutes per side. Serve the pesto on the side, or spooned on top of cooked chicken.

The Day Before:
Bake cake. Make pizza dough, sauté bell peppers for pizza, and grate mozzarella and parmesan cheeses. Store all ingredients in refrigerator until ready to cook. Dice peppers to go with chicken and refrigerate.
Make pesto and refrigerate.

The Day Of:
Make pizza dough and press in pan or pans. Prepare grill. Grill sausage. Remove and let cool about 5 minutes. Add to sautéed peppers and toss. Sprinkle mixture over pizza. Bake pizzas and serve. Remove pesto from refrigerator an hour before you are ready to serve chicken. Grill chicken. When you turn chicken over to second side start to sauté diced peppers.

For the Pesto
2 cups basil leaves
2 large cloves garlic
2 ounces grated parmesan cheese
$^1/_3$ cup extra virgin olive oil
freshly ground black pepper, to taste

*T*ear basil leaves into small pieces and place in bowl of food processor, fitted with a steel blade. Add garlic and parmesan cheese. Process until all ingredients are finely minced. Scrape down sides of processor with rubber spatula. Turn on processor, then slowly, in a thin stream, add olive oil. Blend until fairly smooth. Season with plenty of freshly ground black pepper.

To serve, divide the sautéed peppers equally between 8 plates. Place the chicken on top of the peppers and top with the pesto. Garnish each plate with 2 basil leaves.

Makes about $^3/_4$ cup pesto
Serves 8

GREAT
GRILLING

Grilled Chicken Salad with Mandarin Oranges

Grilled Coho Salmon with Saffron and Tomato Vinaigrette

Steamed Broccoli

Pommes Frites

White Chocolate Mousse

Wine: Meurseault

GRILLED CHICKEN SALAD WITH MANDARIN ORANGES

2 8-ounce boneless chicken breasts cut into
    2-inch strips
1/2 cup freshly squeezed orange juice
1/4 cup champagne vinegar
grated rind from one navel orange
1/2 cup extra virgin olive oil
salt and freshly ground black pepper, to taste
3 small Mandarin oranges, peeled, sectioned,
    and seeded, or 1 8-ounce can Mandarin
    orange sections
1 bunch watercress
1 small head red leaf lettuce

*I*n a medium-sized bowl, combine orange juice, vinegar, orange rind, oil, and salt and pepper to taste. In another medium-sized bowl, add the chicken strips and pour all but 3 tablespoons of the marinade over the chicken. Toss to coat and allow to marinate in refrigerator, covered with plastic wrap, for 3 hours. Reserve remaining dressing for salad greens; keep this dressing at room temperature.

Prepare grill.

Wash lettuce and trim watercress. Tear lettuce into bite size pieces. Add watercress and reserve greens in large mixing bowl.

Grill chicken strips over high heat about 2 to 3 minutes on each side. Pour the remaining 3 tablespoons marinade over the greens. Toss and divide greens evenly among 6 plates. Place two grilled strips on each plate. Garnish with Mandarin orange sections. Season with more freshly ground black pepper. Serve at room temperature.

Makes 1 cup marinade
Serves 6

© Michael Grand 1989

GRILLED

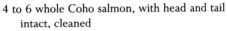

COHO SALMON

WITH SAFFRON

AND TOMATO

VINAIGRETTE

PERFECT TIMING

The Day Before:
Make white chocolate mousse up to two days in advance.

4 to 6 whole Coho salmon, with head and tail
  intact, cleaned
2 heaping teaspoons Dijon-style mustard
1 teaspoon saffron threads
1 small shallot, minced
¼ cup champagne vinegar or white wine
  vinegar
½ cup vegetable oil
2 medium plum tomatoes, seeded and cut into
  ½-inch chunks
salt and freshly ground black pepper, to taste
1 bunch watercress

Prepare the grill. Season the salmon with salt and black pepper inside the cavity and out. Brush both sides of each fish with vegetable oil. Grill salmon over medium-high heat for about 5 to 7 minutes per side or until flesh is opaque and flakes away from the bone.

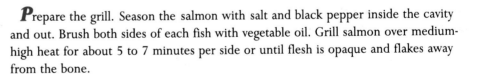

The Day Of:

Marinate chicken tenderloins 3 hours before ready to grill. Clean salad greens. Place in resealable plastic bag in refrigerator. Make saffron and tomato vinaigrette up to 2 hours in advance and allow to sit at room temperature. Trim broccoli. Julienne potatoes, then keep in cold water. Drain and dry with paper towels before frying. Prepare grill. Heat oil for frying potatoes. Fry potatoes, drain on paper towels, remove to an oven-proof serving dish and keep warm in oven. Grill chicken. While chicken is grilling, set up plates with salad. Grill salmon. Put pot of small amount of salted water on stove and bring to a boil. 10 minutes before salmon is cooked, steam broccoli.

While fish is cooking, prepare vinaigrette. In the bowl of a food processor, fitted with a steel blade, combine mustard, saffron, shallot, and vinegar. Blend well. With processor still running, add oil slowly, in a thin stream. Add tomatoes and continue to process until tomatoes are well chopped. Season with salt and black pepper to taste.

To serve, place a small amount of vinaigrette in the center of 4 to 6 plates. Swirl each plate around until the sauce spreads to the edge of the plate. Place grilled salmon in center and garnish with a small bunch of watercress.

Makes about 1 1/2 cups vinaigrette
Serves 4 to 6

Sliced Tomato Salad
with Cumin, Oil,
and Vinegar

■ *Hot Indian
Shrimp*

Brown Basmati Rice

*Yellow Squash Sauté
with Ground
Coriander*

Flan

Ceylon Tea

*Wine:
Sauvignon Blanc*

HOT INDIAN

SHRIMP

2 large cloves garlic
1 2-inch piece fresh ginger, peeled
1/2 teaspoon fennel seeds
1 tablespoon ground cumin
1 teaspoon coriander seeds
2 teaspoons hot Hungarian paprika
1/2 teaspoons salt
1 cup plain low fat yogurt
1/2 cup freshly squeezed lime juice
2 1/2 pounds large shrimp

PERFECT TIMING
The Day Before:
Make flan. Make marinade for shrimp and refrigerate. Make vinaigrette for tomatoes. Clean shrimp and refrigerate. Clean yellow squash and slice into 1-inch slices and then into quarters.

The Day Of:
If using bamboo skewers, soak for 1/2 hour. Slice tomatoes. Prepare grill. Cook rice. 10 minutes before rice is cooked, add shrimp to grill. Remove shrimp when done and keep warm in oven, if necessary. 5 minutes before shrimp are done, heat sauté pan and add oil. Sauté squash and season with coriander.

*I*n the bowl of a food processor fitted with a steel blade, combine garlic, ginger, fennel seeds, cumin, coriander seeds, paprika, and salt. Blend for 2 to 3 minutes until most of the seeds have been crushed. Add yogurt and lime juice and blend until smooth. Scrape mixture into large bowl and set aside.

Using a small set of sharp kitchen scissors, cut legs off shrimp. Cut each shell down the back to the last segment and pull out the intestinal vein. Loosen the shells slightly without removing them, so that the marinade can penetrate. Rinse shrimp and pat dry with paper towel. Add shrimp to yogurt marinade. Cover and refrigerate 3 hours.

Prepare grill. Skewer shrimp. When heat is medium high, place skewers on grill. Cook until shells are slightly charred and shrimp is opaque and moist, about 3 to 5 minutes per side. Serve with plenty of fresh lime wedges.

Serves 4 to 6

NOTE: If you cannot fit all the skewers on the grill at one time, make certain to scrape down the grill with a wire brush before putting on more skewers since the yogurt marinade will stick to the grid.

© Michael Grand 1989

© Guy Powers/Envision

GREAT
GRILLING

Cold Cucumber, Yogurt, and Dill Soup

■ *Marinated Grilled Duck Breast Salad with Fresh Raspberries*

Lemon Sorbet

Espresso

Wine: Gewürtztraminer

MARINATED GRILLED DUCK BREAST SALAD WITH FRESH RASPBERRIES

For the Duck
3 whole duck breasts, about 10 ounces each
1 teaspoon chopped fresh thyme leaves
1 teaspoon pink peppercorns, crushed
$1/4$ cup raspberry vinegar
1 tablespoon Dijon-style mustard
$1/2$ cup safflower oil
$1/4$ cup hazelnut oil
$1/2$ teaspoon salt
freshly ground black pepper, to taste

Cut each duck breast in half. With a small sharp knife make approximately 3 diagonal slashes in the skin making certain not to pierce the meat. Place the breasts in a shallow glass or ceramic dish and reserve.

In a small mixing bowl, combine thyme, peppercorns, vinegar, and mustard. Blend thoroughly with a wire whisk. Continue beating mixture with wire whisk while adding oils in a thin stream until mixture is well emulsified. Add salt and black pepper to taste.

Pour $3/4$ cup of the marinade over the duck breasts and toss to coat. Reserve remaining $1/4$ cup dressing for salad greens. Cover duck with plastic wrap and refrigerate for 4 to 6 hours. Remove from refrigerator one half hour before grilling.

The Day Before:
Make the soup up to a day in advance. You can also make the vinaigrette. Store, covered, in refrigerator until ready to use.

The Day Of:
Marinate the duck breasts. Cook turnips. Store in resealable plastic bag at room temperature. Clean and prepare salad. Store in resealable plastic bag and refrigerate. Prepare grill. Grill duck. While the duck is cooking, toss salad with vinaigrette and arrange on individual plates. Slice the turnips and use as garnish.

For the Salad
1/2 pound mache*
1 small head radicchio
3 endive
1 pound white turnips, peeled, sliced into
    1/4-inch rounds, and boiled
1 pint fresh raspberries

Clean lettuces and tear into bite size pieces. Toss together in a large mixing bowl. Carefully pull leaves from endive and reserve.

Prepare grill. Place duck on grill over medium-high heat, skin side down. Cover and grill 7 to 10 minutes. Turn over to second side and grill an additional 7 to 10 minutes or until desired doneness. Remove cooked ducks to warm platter and allow them to sit 5 minutes before slicing. Slice duck breast halves on the bias into paper thin slices making sure to keep the shape of the breast intact.

Dress salad with remaining 1/2 cup vinaigrette and toss to coat. To serve, put a few endive spears at the top of the plate. Place a small handful of salad in the center of each plate. Fan slices of one half duck breast per plate below salad. Arrange turnip slices on either side of salad greens, and toss a few fresh raspberries over all.

Serves 6

*Mache is also known as corn salad or lambs ear. It is a green grown hydroponically, and it is available in specialty food stores. If you cannot find mache, you can use Bibb lettuce.

ADDITIONAL GREAT GRILLING RECIPES

- *Chicken Salad South of the Border*
- *Classic Barbecued Chicken Wings*
- *Thai-Style Sirloin Burgers*
- *Orange Marmalade and Ginger Glaze*
- *Light Tonnato Sauce for Grilled Veal*
- *Charred Steak Aioli*
- *New Potatoes on Rosemary Skewers*

CHICKEN SALAD SOUTH OF THE BORDER

1/2 cup freshly squeezed lime juice
1/4 cup extra virgin olive oil
1 heaping tablespoon chili mustard, or
    1 teaspoon Dijon-style mustard and
    1 teaspoon hot chili paste
1 teaspoon honey
1 teaspoon salt
2 large jalapeño peppers, seeded and chopped
3 whole chicken breasts, boneless and skinless,
    cut in half
1 quart safflower oil
6 to 8 fresh corn tortillas
1/4 cup chopped fresh cilantro
1/2 cup red wine vinegar
1 large tomato, coarsely chopped
1 large head Romaine lettuce, shredded
2 small Haas avocadoes, cut into thirds thinly
    sliced and spread into a fan shape
2 limes cut into thin wedges

*I*n a large mixing bowl, combine lime juice, olive oil, mustard(s), honey, salt, and jalapeños. Mix until well blended. Add chicken breasts and toss to coat. Let sit at room temperature for 1 hour.

While chicken marinates, place a heavy duty 4-quart (4-liter) saucepot over high heat and add the safflower oil. When oil reaches 350 degrees F. (175 degrees C.) on a deep fat fry thermometer, fry tortillas by placing each tortilla in a double fry basket or in 2 ladles, one inserted inside another. Place the tortilla in the largest fry basket or ladle. Gently press smaller fry basket or ladle into center of tortilla to get basket shape. Immerse both baskets with tortilla into the hot oil. Remove baskets once torilla takes shape, but continue basting with hot oil to cook through. Let tortilla fry until golden brown, about 2 to 3 minutes. Remove cooked tortilla basket from hot oil and drain on paper towels. Continue this process, cooking the tortillas one at a time until all the baskets are made.

Prepare grill. Grill chicken breast halves over high heat. Cover with grill lid or aluminum foil tent. Cook about 7 to 10 minutes on each side or until golden brown and cooked through. Remove from grill to cutting board. Let sit about 10 minutes. Tear chicken into thin strips and place in a medium sized mixing bowl. Add cilantro and red wine vinegar and toss thoroughly.

Assemble salad by placing a small handful of lettuce on the bottom of each plate. Sprinkle about 1 tablespoon chopped tomato over lettuce. Place cup-shaped tortilla in center of plate and fill with about 1 cup of chicken salad. Garnish plate with thinly sliced avocado and lime wedges.

Serves 4 to 6

CLASSIC BARBECUED CHICKEN WINGS

2 tablespoons extra virgin olive oil
1 medium onion, finely chopped
4 large cloves garlic, minced
1/2 cup ketchup
1/4 cup cider vinegar
2 tablespoons dark brown sugar
2 tablespoons freshly squeezed lemon juice
1 teaspoon salt
2 tablespoons chili mustard, or 2 tablespoons
    Dijon-style mustard and 2 teaspoons hot
    chili paste
1 tablespoon hot chili powder
1 teaspoon hot red pepper sauce
12 to 14 chicken wings

*I*n a 3-quart (3-liter) saucepan over medium-high heat, add olive oil. When hot, add onion. Stir constantly with a wooden spoon until onion is transparent, about 1 to 2 minutes. Add garlic and stir 30 seconds. Reduce heat to medium. Add ketchup, vinegar, sugar, lemon juice, salt, chili mustard, chili powder, and hot red pepper sauce. Bring sauce to boil. Remove from heat. Add chicken wings to large mixing bowl. Pour barbecue sauce over chicken and stir to coat.

Prepare grill. Grill chicken wings over medium-high heat, turning once or twice, for about 15 to 20 minutes or until skin is slightly charred and juices run clear.

Serves 4 to 6 as appetizer

© Michael Grand 1989

For The Burgers

2 pounds ground sirloin
2 teaspoons Wasabi powder
1 2-inch piece ginger, peeled and grated
2 large cloves garlic, minced
2 tablespoons low sodium soy sauce
1/2 cup scallions, minced
2 teaspoons granulated sugar
salt and pepper, to taste
8 large Boston lettuce leaves
1/2 cup coriander leaves
1/2 cup mint leaves
1/2 cup cooked short-grained white rice

*P*reheat the grill to high. Combine the sirloin, Wasabi, ginger, garlic, soy sauce, scallions, sugar, and salt and pepper in a medium-sized mixing bowl. Mix well until blended. Shape into 4 8-ounce patties. When heat is high, cook hamburgers until desired doneness.

For the Sauce

1/4 cup white wine vinegar
1 teaspoon Hoisin sauce
1 teaspoon soy bean paste
2 large cloves garlic, crushed
2 teaspoons low sodium soy sauce
1/2 teaspoon hot red pepper flakes

*I*n a small mixing bowl, combine all ingredients and blend well. Makes 1/2 cup sauce.

To serve, wrap one or two lettuce leaves around a patty. Spoon about 1 tablespoon each fresh coriander, mint, and cooked rice into the lettuce envelope and wrap to seal. Dip into spicy vinegar sauce.

Serves 4

ORANGE MARMALADE AND GINGER GLAZE FOR PORK SPARERIBS

2 tablespoons sesame oil
6 large cloves garlic, peeled and crushed
1 3-inch piece fresh ginger, peeled and grated
$^1/_3$ cup tamari or low sodium soy sauce
$^1/_4$ cup rice wine vinegar
4 whole cloves
1 2-inch piece cinnamon stick
$^1/_4$ cup low sugar orange marmalade preserves
salt and freshly ground black pepper, to taste

Combine all of the above ingredients in a 1-quart (1-liter) saucepot and bring to a boil over high heat, stirring constantly. Reduce heat to medium and let simmer 2 to 3 minutes. Remove from heat and allow the glaze to cool to room temperature. Season glaze with salt and black pepper. Before grilling ribs, generously coat them with the sauce.

Makes about 1 cup glaze

LIGHT TONNATO SAUCE FOR GRILLED VEAL

1 cup dry white wine
1 cup chicken broth or stock
1 6$^1/_2$-ounce can tuna, packed in water, drained
6 canned anchovy fillets
1 tablespoon anchovy oil, from can
2 cloves garlic
$^1/_4$ cup olive oil

2 tablespoons capers
2 tablespoons freshly squeezed lemon juice
2 tablespoons low calorie mayonnaise
freshly ground black pepper, to taste

*I*n a 2-quart (2-liter) saucepan, over high heat, combine dry white wine and chicken broth. Bring to boil. Reduce heat to medium and allow liquid to reduce by half, about 10 minutes. Remove from heat and reserve.

In the bowl of a food processor fitted with a steel blade, combine tuna, anchovy fillets, anchovy oil, and garlic. Process until mixture is smooth. Slowly add olive oil and reduced wine and broth. Add capers, lemon juice, and mayonnaise, and continue to process until well blended. Season sauce with plenty of freshly ground black pepper. Use at room temperature or refrigerated. Serve with hot or cold grilled veal chops.

Makes about 2 cups sauce

CHARRED STEAK

WITH AIOLI

5 to 8 large cloves garlic
2 large egg yolks
1/2 cup extra virgin olive oil
2 tablespoons sherry wine vinegar
salt and freshly ground black pepper, to taste
2 tablespoons chopped parsley
1 3-pound sirloin steak, about 2-inches thick

*I*n the bowl of a food processor fitted with a steel blade, combine garlic and egg yolks and blend until garlic is finely chopped. Stop the processor from time to time to scrape down the sides of the bowl. With processor running, slowly add olive oil in a thin stream. When well blended, add vinegar, salt, pepper, and parsley. Stir. If not cooking steak immediately, cover Aioli with plastic wrap and refrigerate.

Prepare grill. Sear steak over high heat for 3 to 5 minutes on each side to seal in juices. Remove to medium-high heat and continue to grill until desired doneness. Remove cooked steak to cutting board and let stand 10 minutes. Slice very thinly and serve with the Aioli sauce on the side.

Makes about 1/2 cup sauce
Serves 8 to 10

NEW POTATOES

ON ROSEMARY

SKEWERS

2 pounds red skinned potatoes
2 large bunches rosemary
extra virgin olive oil
2 large cloves garlic, crushed
salt and freshly ground black pepper, to taste

*I*n a 2-quart (2-liter) saucepan, add potatoes and enough cold, salted water, to cover. Bring to boil over high heat. Cook about 15 to 20 minutes until tender but firm. Drain in colander and cool completely. DO NOT RINSE! When potatoes are cooled carefully poke skewer through potato from top to bottom. Remove skewer and replace with sprig of rosemary. You should be able to put at least 2 potatoes on each sprig. Generously coat potatoes with olive oil. Rub crushed garlic over all, and season with salt and freshly ground black pepper to taste.

Prepare grill. Grill potatoes over medium heat for about 10 to 15 minutes, rotating occasionally to insure even cooking. Outsides of potatoes should be slightly charred.

Serves 4 to 6

- *HERB BUTTER*

- *SPICY GREEN BUTTER*

- *PROVENÇAL BUTTER*

- *DILL, BLACK OLIVE, AND PIMIENTO BUTTER*

- *ANCHOVY BUTTER*

- *SMOKED SALMON BUTTER*

HERB BUTTER

For grilled beef, lamb, and veal
1 stick sweet butter, softened to room temperature
2 teaspoons chopped fresh tarragon
1 teaspoon chopped fresh basil
2 tablespoons chopped Italian leaf parsley
1 tablespoon chopped fresh thyme leaves
2 teaspoons brandy
$^{1}/_{2}$ teaspoon salt
plenty of freshly ground black pepper

Cream the butter. Blend in tarragon, basil, parsley, thyme, brandy, salt, and black pepper.

Makes $^{1}/_{2}$ cup

SPICY GREEN BUTTER

For grilled chicken and red snapper
1 stick sweet butter, softened to room temperature
1 tablespoon snipped chives
1 small jalapeño pepper, seeded and finely minced
1 tablespoon freshly squeezed lime juice
$^{1}/_{4}$ cup chopped cilantro
$^{1}/_{4}$ teaspoon salt

Cream the butter. Blend in chives, jalapeño, lime juice, cilantro, and salt.

Makes $^{1}/_{2}$ cup

PROVENÇAL

BUTTER

For Grilled Chicken, Fish, Veal, Vegetables, and Beef

1 stick sweet butter, softened to room
    temperature
1 large clove garlic, crushed
2 large plum tomatoes, peeled, seeded, and
    finely chopped
1/4 cup fresh basil, finely minced
1/4 teaspoon salt
1/4 tablespoon freshly ground black pepper

Cream the butter. Blend in garlic, tomatoes, basil, salt, and pepper.

Makes 1 cup

DILL,

BLACK OLIVE, AND

PIMIENTO BUTTER

For Grilled Pork, Chicken, and Fish Steaks

1 stick sweet butter, softened to room
    temperature
1/4 cup chopped fresh dill
15 niçoise olives, pitted and finely chopped
2 tablespoons chopped pimientos
salt and black pepper, to taste

Cream the butter. Blend in dill, olives, pimientoes, salt, and pepper.

Makes 1 cup

ANCHOVY BUTTER

For Grilled Veal, Chicken, and Swordfish
1 stick sweet butter, softened to room
    temperature
3 anchovy fillets, minced
1 large shallot, minced
1 tablespoon freshly squeezed lemon juice
$1/4$ teaspoon ground white pepper
1 tablespoon chopped parsley

Cream the butter. Blend in anchovies, garlic, shallot, lemon juice, pepper, and parsley.

Makes $1/2$ cup

SMOKED SALMON

BUTTER

For Grilled Fish
1 stick sweet butter, softened to room
    temperature
2 ounces smoked Nova Scotia salmon, chopped
    in food processor
1 tablespoon freshly squeezed lemon juice
black pepper to taste

Cream the butter. Blend in smoked salmon, lemon juice, and black pepper to taste.

Makes $1/2$ cup

TO SERVE BUTTERS

*A*fter butter is mixed, place it in the center of a 12″ by 12″ (30 cm by 30 cm) square of wax paper. Shape into a log and roll up in wax paper. Twist both ends to make tight roll shape and refrigerate until firm. Fifteen minutes before grilled food is cooked, remove butter from refrigerator. Slice into $1/4$-inch ($1/2$-centimeter) rounds, remove wax paper, and place on top of grilled meat. Let melt for a few seconds before serving.

LIQUID MEASURE EQUIVALENTS

3 teaspoons = 1 tablespoon

2 tablespoons = 1 fluid ounce

4 tablespoons = $\frac{1}{4}$ cup = 2 fluid ounces

5 tablespoons + 1 teaspoon = $\frac{1}{3}$ cup = $2\frac{2}{3}$ ounces

8 tablespoons = $\frac{1}{2}$ cup = 4 fluid ounces

10 tablespoons = $\frac{2}{3}$ cup

12 tablespoons = $\frac{3}{4}$ cup

16 tablespoons = 1 cup = 8 fluid ounces

2 cups = 16 fluid ounces = 1 pint

4 cups = 32 fluid ounces = 1 quart

8 cups = 64 fluid ounces = $\frac{1}{2}$ gallon

4 quarts = 128 fluid ounces = 1 gallon

METRIC CONVERSION TABLE

TO CHANGE	TO	MULTIPLY BY
teaspoons	milliliters	5
tablespoons	milliliters	15
fluid ounces	milliliters	30
ounces	grams	28
cups	liters	0.24
pints	liters	0.47
quarts	liters	0.95
gallons	liters	3.8
pounds	kilograms	0.45
inches	centimeters	2.5

To change Fahrenheit temperature to Celsius temperature, subtract 32, multiply by 5 then divide by 9.

GENERAL INFORMATION

The Barbecue Industry of America
Myers Communi Counsel
11 Penn Plaza
New York, NY 10001

BARBECUES, TOOLS, AND ACCESSORIES

Charbroil
W.C. Bradley Enterprises
P.O. Box 1240
Columbus, GA 31902

Christen Incorporated
59 Branch Street
Saint Louis, MI 63147

Community Kitchens Coffee Company
P.O. Box 3778
Baton Rouge, LA 70821

Ducane
800 Dutch Square Boulevard
Columbia, SC 29210

Malibu 326
T.M. Anova Incorporated
P.O. Box 6000
Barrie, ONT L4M 4V3
CANADA

Meco
P.O. Box 1000 (1500 Industrial Road)
Greenville, TN 37744

Nordic Gas Grills
Division of Northland Aluminum Products
Highway 7 at 100
Minneapolis, MN 55416

Shepherd Products Limited
8016 Kennedy Road
Markham, ONT L3R 2E4
CANADA

Sunbeam
Howard Bush Drive
Neosho, MI 64850

The Terrace Group
16 Westwood Avenue
Rumford, Rhode Island 02916
High performance, outdoor charcoal grills.

Thermos
Route 75
Freeport, IL 61032

Weber
Weber-Stephen Products Company
200 East Daniels Road
Palatine, IL 60067

Zona
97 Greene Street
New York, NY 10013

CHARCOAL, WOOD AND CHIPS

Barbecue Wood Flavors
1701 Oak Grove Road
Ennis, TX 75119

Flying " W" Wood Products
Box 1301
Brady, TX 76825
Mesquite and hickory wood

Imperial Products Corporation
1850 Craigshire Plaza
Suite 204
St. Louis, MO 63146

The Kingsford Company
1221 Broadway
Oakland, CA 96412

Nordic Gas Grills
Division of Northland Aluminum Products
Highway 7 at 100
Minneapolis, MN 55416

Peoples Gourmet Woods
55 Mill Street
Cumberland, Rhode Island 02864
*All natural grill fuels including lump
hardwood charcoals and fruitwoods
for flavoring.*

The Spice Hunter
850-C Capitolio Way
San Luis Obispo, CA 93401

Tennessee Traditions
Jack Daniels Charcoal
P.O. Box 1669
Brentwood, TN 37027

Turkey Hill Farm
RD 1
Box 163
Red Hook, NY 12571

Weber
Weber-Stephen
200 East Daniels Road
Palatine, IL 60067

Western Smokin' Chips
W.W. Wood, Inc.
P.O. Box 244
Pleasanton, TX 78064

MAIL ORDER GOURMET FOODS

Balducci's
424 Sixth Avenue
New York, NY 10011

The Chef's Catalogue
3915 Commercial Avenue
Northbrook, IL 60062

Community Kitchens Company
P.O. Box 3778
Baton Route, LA 70821

Lloyd Harbor Greens
Gerry Lane
RFD 1
Lloyd Harbor, NY 11743

Williams-Sonoma
Mail Order Department
P.O. Box 7456
San Francisco, CA 94120

Zabar's
249 West 80th Street
New York, NY 10024

INDEX

A

Accessories, 20-26
Aioli, steak with, 119
Alder, 19
Aluminum foil, 22
Anchovy Butter, 123
Appetizers
  barbecued chicken wings, 116
  marinated peppers, 63
Apricots, and peach chutney, veal chops with, 85-86
Arugula, salmon with salsa cruda and, 55-57

B

Baby Back Pork Ribs with Mocha Java Barbecue Sauce, 43-44
Barbecue sauce, mocha java pork ribs with, 43-44
Barbecued Squab, 46-47
Basil
  pesto, paillard of chicken with, 104-105
  and pine nuts, polenta with, 50-51
  and tomatoes and garlic, fennel with, 79
Basting brushes, 23, 25-26
Beans, black, crabs and ginger with, 74-75
Beef
  Thai-style sirloin burgers, 117
  See also Steak
Berries, raspberries, duck salad with, 113-114
Black beans, crabs with, and ginger, 74-75
Blood orange butter sauce, swordfish in, 89-91
Boneless Loin Lambchops with Port Wine Sauce, 64-65
Brushes, 23, 25-26
Burgers, Thai-style sirloin, 117
Butter
  anchovy, 123
  blood orange sauce, swordfish in, 89-91
  dill, black olive, and pimiento, 122
  herb, 121
  Provençal, 122
  to serve, 123
  smoked salmon, 123
  spicy green, 121

C

Carving boards, 24-25
Charcoal, 18
  laying to fire, 30-31
  starters, 21-22
Charcoal Grilled Lobster with Coral and Tamale Vinaigrette, 81
Charred Steak with Aioli, 119
Cheese, mozzarella, and veal sausage and pepper pizza, 102-3

Chicken
  barbecued wings, 116
  paillard, with pesto, 104-5
  salad
    with mandarin oranges, 107
    South of the Border, 115-16
    with sundried tomatoes, garlic, and pasta, 93-94
  yaketori, 61
Chicken Salad South of the Border, 115-116
Chicken Yaketori, 61
Chile, and mint dressing
  leg of lamb with, 82-83
  pork salad with, 70-71
Chutney, peach and apricot, veal chops with, 85-86
Circular grills, 12
Citrus peels, swordfish grilled over, 89-91
Classic Barbecued Chicken Wings, 116
Cooking fuel, 18-20
Coral and tamale vinaigrette, lobster with, 81
Corn, on cob, grilled, 45
Cornish game hens, spiced, 53
Crabs, with ginger and black beans, 74-75
Cumin-Marinated Lamb Kebobs, 101

D

Dill, Black Olive, and Pimiento Butter, 122
Disposable grills, 11
Dressings
  chile and mint
    leg of lamb with, 82-83
    pork salad with, 70-71
  See also Butter; Sauces
Drip pans, 24
Duck, salad, with raspberries 113-14

E

Eggplant, with sesame sauce, 52
Electric grills, 14-15

F

Fajites, 59
Fennel, with tomato, basil, and garlic, 79
Fire
  laying for, 30-31
  temperature of, 31
Fire starter chimneys, 20-21
Fireside Quail, 67
Fish and seafood
  general cooking times, 39
  grilling tips for, 35-36
  shellfish. See specific shellfish
  See also specific fish and seafood
Flavor chips, 27
Fruit wood fuels, 20
Fruits. See specific fruits
Fuel, 18-20

G

Game and game birds
  cornish game hens, spiced, 53
  quail, 67
  venison, in red wine marinade, 49
Garlic
  aioli, steak with, 119
  and sundried tomatoes in pasta, chicken with, 93-94
  and tomatoes and basil, fennel with, 79
Gas grills, 14-15
Ginger
  crabs with, and black beans, 74-75
  and orange marmalade glaze, for spareribs, 118
Glazes, orange marmalade and ginger, for spareribs, 118
Grapevine fuels, 20
Grilled Boneless Leg of Lamb with Chiles and Mint, 82-83
Grilled Mexican Salad with Mandarin Oranges, 107
Grilled Chicken with Sundried Tomatoes, Garlic, and Fusilli Pasta, 93-94
Grilled Coho Salmon with Saffron and Tomato Vinaigrette, 109-110
Grilled Corn on the Cob, 45
Grilled Eggplant with Sesame Sauce, 52
Grilled Fennel with Tomato, Basil, and Garlic, 79
Grilled Leeks Vinaigrette, 95-96
Grilled Marinated Pepper Appetizer, 63
Grilled Mixed Baby Vegetables, 87
Grilled Polenta with Pine Nuts and Basil, 50-51
Grilled Pork Tenderloin in Black Soy and Rock Candy Marinade, 76-77
Grilled Red Onion Slices, 69
Grilled Salmon with Salsa Cruda and Sautéed Arugula, 55-57
Grilled Sea Scallops with Pecans and Tarragon Vin Blanc Sauce, 99-100
Grilled Soft Shell Crabs with Ginger and Black Beans, 74-75
Grilled Spiced Cornish Game Hens, 53
Grilled Veal Chops with Peach and Apricot Chutney, 85-86
Grilled Veal Sausage, Pepper, and Mozzarella Cheese Pizza, 102-3
Grilled Venison Steaks in Red Wine Marinade, 49
Grilled Vietnamese Pork Salad with Mint and Chile Dressing, 70-71
Grilled Wild Mushrooms, 66

Grilling baskets, 27-28
Grills
  accessories for, 20-26
  cleaning, 37
  fuel for, 18-20
  renting of, 17
  seasoning, 37
  types, 10-17

H

Hamburgers, Thai-style sirloin, 117
Hardwood charcoal, 18
Herb Butter, 121
Herb-Grilled Trout, 97
Herbs and spices
  butter, 121
  in cooking fuels, 20
  grilled trout, 97
  See also specific herbs and spices
Hibachis, 10-11
Hickory, 19
Hooded grills, 13
Hot Indian Shrimp, 111

J

Japanese Marinated Grilled Tuna Steak, 68

K

Kamados, 14
Kettles, 12-13
Knives, 22

L

Lamb
  chops, with Port wine sauce, 64-65
  grilling tips for, 34
  kebobs, cumin-marinated, 101
  leg of, with chiles and mint, 82-83
Leeks, vinaigrette, 95-96
Lemon Shrimp, 72-73
Light Tonnato Sauce for Grilled Veal, 118-19
Liquid measure equivalents, 124
Lobster, with coral and tamale vinaigrette, 81

M

Marinades
  black soy and rock candy, pork tenderloin in, 76-77
  cumin, lamb kebobs, 101
  duck breast salad, with raspberries, 113-14
  pepper appetizer, 63
  red wine, venison in, 49
  for tuna steak, 68
Marinated Grilled Duck Breast Salad with Fresh Raspberries, 113-14
Marmalade, glaze with ginger, for spareribs, 118
Measure equivalents, 124
Meat
  game. See Game and game birds

general cooking times, 39
grilling tips, 32-35
steak. See Steak
testing for doneness, 32, 38
See also specific types of meat
Mesquite, 18-19
Metric conversion, 124
Mint, and chile dressing
  leg of lamb with, 82-83
  pork salad with, 70-71
Mitts, 25
Mixed vegetables
  grilled, 87
  See also specific vegetables
Mozzarella cheese, and veal sausage and pepper pizza, 102-3
Mushrooms, 66

N

New Potatoes on Rosemary Skewers, 120
Nuts,
  pecans, scallops with tarragon vin blanc sauce and, 99-100
  pine, polenta with basil and, 50-51

O

Olives, and dill and pimiento butter, 122
Onions, red, grilled slices, 69
Orange Marmalade and Ginger Glaze for Pork Spareribs, 118
Oranges
  butter sauce, swordfish in, 89-91
  mandarin, chicken salad with, 107
  marmalade glaze with ginger, for spareribs, 118

P

Pads, 25
Paillard of Chicken with Light Pesto, 104-05
Pasta, and garlic and sundried tomatoes, chicken with 93-94
Peaches, and apricot chutney, veal chops with, 85-86
Pecans, and tarragon vin blanc sauce, scallops with, 99-100
Peppers
  marinated, 63
  and veal sausage and mozzarella cheese pizza, 102-3
Pesto, paillard of chicken with, 104-5
Pimientos, and olive and dill butter, 122
Pine nuts, and basil, polenta with, 50-51
Pizza, veal sausage, pepper, and mozzarella cheese, 102-3

Polenta, with pine nuts and
basil, 50-51
Pork
grilling tips for, 34
ribs, with Mocha Java
barbecue sauce, 43-44
salad, with mint and chile
dressing, 70-71
spareribs, orange marmalade
and ginger glaze for, 118
tenderloin, in soy and rock
candy marinade, 76-77
Potatoes, on rosemary skewers, 120
Poultry
general cooking times, 39
grilling tips for, 34-35
*See also specific types of
poultry; Game and game birds*
Provençal Butter, 122

Q
Quail, 67

R
Raspberries, duck salad with, 113-14
Rock candy, and soy marinade,
pork tenderloin in,
76-77
Rosemary, skewed potatoes, 120

S
Saffron, and tomato
vinaigrette, salmon
with, 109-10
Salads
chicken
with mandarin oranges, 107
South of the Border,
115-16
duck, with raspberries,
113-14
pork, with mint and chile
dressing, 70-71
Salmon
with saffron and tomato
vinaigrette, 109-10
with salsa cruda and
arugula, 55-57
smoked, butter, 123
Salsa cruda, salmon with, and
arugula, 55-57
Sauces
blood orange butter,
swordfish in, 89-91
Port wine, lambchops with,
64-65
salsa cruda, salmon with,
55-57
sesame, eggplant with, 52
tarragon vin blanc, scallops
with pecans and, 99-100
tonnato, for veal, 118-19
See also Butter; Dressings
Sausage, veal, and pepper and
mozzarella cheese pizza,
102-3
Scallops, with pecans and
tarragon vin blanc
sauce, 99-100

Seafood. *See specific types
of fish and seafood;*
Fish and seafood
Service spoons, 23
Sesame sauce, eggplant with, 52
Sesame Swordfish Kebobs, 62
Shrimp
hot Indian, 111
lemon, 72-73
Sirloin burgers, Thai-style, 117
Skewers, 23
Smoked Salmon Butter, 123
Smokers, 16-17
Smoking chips, 27
Soy, and rock candy marinade,
pork tenderloin in,
76-77
Spareribs, orange marmalade,
and ginger glaze for, 118
Spatulas, 22
Spicy Green Butter, 121
Spit roasting equipment, 26
Spray bottles, 22-23
Squab, barbecued, 46-47
Steak
with aioli, 119
fajites, 59
grilling method, 33
Swordfish
with blood orange butter
sauce, 89-91
sesame kebobs, 62
Swordfish Grilled over Citrus
Peels with Blood Orange
Butter Sauce, 89-91

T
Tarragon, vin blanc sauce
scallops with pecans
and, 99-100
Thai-Style Sirloin Burgers, 117
Thermometers, 24, 26
Tomatoes
and basil and garlic, fennel
with, 79
and saffron vinaigrette,
salmon with, 109-110
sundried, chicken with,
93-94
Tongs, 25
Tonnato sauce, for veal, 118-119
Trout, herb-grilled, 97
Tuna, steak, marinated, 68

U
Utensils, 20-26

V
Veal
chops, with peach and
apricot chutney, 85-86
grilling tips for, 34
sausage, and pepper and
mozzarella cheese pizza,
102-3
tonnato sauce for, 118-19

Vegetables
grilled mixed, 87
grilling tips for, 36
*See also specific
vegetables*
Venison, grilled steaks, in
red wine marinade, 49
Vinaigrettes
coral and tamale, lobster
with, 81
leeks, 95-96
saffron and tomato, salmon,
with, 109-10

W
Wheeled grills, 12
Wild mushrooms, 66
Wine
marinades, venison steaks
in, 49
sauce
lambchops with, 64-65
scallops with pecans and,
99-100

Photography Credits for Silhouetted Photgraphs

© A.G.E. Fotostock/FPG International:
35, 46, 95

© R. Chandler/FPG International: 105

Courtesy Christen, Inc.: 26

Courtesy Crate & Barrel: 27

© John Dominis/Wheeler Pictures:
14-15, 32-33, 44-45, 64, 71, 73, 83,
102, 118

© Michael Grand: 34, 37, 43, 44, 47,
56, 61, 62, 63, 66-67, 71, 72, 75,
77, 80-81, 86-87, 89, 93, 103, 104,
107, 115, 116-117, 120

© Lynn Karlin: 36

© R. Laird/FPG International: 50

© Robert Lima/Envision: 96,108-109

© T. Lindley/FPG International: 52-53

© Melabee M. Miller/Envision: 59

© Jeffry W. Myers/FPG International: 67

© Steven Mark Needham/Envision:
104-105

© Amy Reichman/Envision: 70-71

© F. Stein/FPG International: 97

© Courtesy Sunbeam, Inc.: 10-11,
12-13, 14

© Tom Tracy/FPG International: 114

© Von Nordeck/FPG International:
24-25

Courtesy Williams-Sonoma: 16